Katherine
Hear "
- rele            ar!

# THE SOUND OF HEAVEN

BY ANDREW MURRAY

The Sound of Heaven

Copyright 2019 Andrew Murray

No part of this book may be used or reproduced in any matter without the written permission of the author. This book may not be reprinted without permission from the author.

All Scripture quotations unless otherwise indicated are taken from the Holy Bible, New International Version® Anglicized, NIV® Copyright © 1979, 1984, 2011 by Biblica, Inc.®
Used by permission. All rights reserved worldwide

Scripture taken from the New King James Version®. Copyright © 1982 by Thomas Nelson. Used by permission. All rights reserved.

The Passion Translation®. Copyright © 2017 by Passion & Fire Ministries, Inc.
Used by permission. All rights reserved. thePassionTranslation.com

Scripture taken from The Message. Copyright © 1993, 1994, 1995, 1996, 2000, 2001, 2002. Used by permission of NavPress Publishing Group.

Scripture quotations taken from the Amplified® Bible (AMP),
Copyright © 2015 by The Lockman Foundation
Used by permission. www.Lockman.org

Published by Generation Builders

Book designed and formatted by Laura Murray at Peanut Designs www.pnutd.co.uk

# CONTENTS

| | | |
|---|---|---|
| Foreword: By Jarrod Cooper | | 9 |
| Introduction | | 13 |
| 1. | Can you hear what I hear? | 19 |
| 2. | Listening to the sound | 37 |
| 3. | The sound of invitation | 55 |
| 4. | The sound of revival | 73 |
| 5. | The sound of the imposter | 95 |
| 6. | The sound of blood | 113 |
| 7. | The sound of passion | 131 |
| 8. | The sound of prayer | 149 |
| 9. | The sound of praise | 165 |
| 10. | The alpha and omega of sound | 189 |
| 11. | The sound of the lion and the trumpet | 207 |
| 12. | The sound of the Church | 227 |
| Conclusion: Finding your penguin | | 245 |
| Afterword: The power of praying in tongues | | 251 |

## Acknowledgements

My beautiful wife Laura

Judah and Asher – my boys

The rest of the Murray family – mum and dad, Matthew, Becky and Josiah

Jarrod and Vicky Cooper – our incredible senior leaders. We love and honour you!

All the wonderful leaders and staff at Revive Church and our entire church family – you are our penguins!

All the brilliant pastors, leaders and friends we know from around the world!

Dave and Carolyn, Cleddie and Gaynell

The Generation Builders trustees – Kevin and Janet, Nigel and Angie, Steven and Sharon, Peter and Anna

The wonderful Maggie Carr for her help with proof reading and editing

## Dedication

To Laura. You always know how to hear and release the sound of heaven. You play in time with the heart-beat of God. Your sound changes the atmosphere, causes strongholds to shift and mountains to move. May His glory always rest on the sound that comes from your life.

Suddenly, in an instant, the Lord Almighty will come with thunder and earthquake and great noise, with whirlwind and tempest and flames of a devouring fire"

*- Isaiah 29:5-6*

# Foreward

I have heard the sounds of heaven several times in my life. Some call it the "sound of revival" – a certain extra something, like a sound within the sound, or the echoes of a distant and glorious realm approaching near.

One of the first times I heard this sound was on a trip to Mexico in the 1990's, where I was singing, the guest of a gathering of 6,000 leaders, who were obviously in some state of revival and renewal as a movement. Something much more than the notes I played, or the melodies I sang, invaded that auditorium, and for hour after hour, for several days, thousands of leaders lay weeping, worshipping and at times wailing like Isaiah in God's temple (See Isaiah 6), as the sound within the sound swirled through the crowd, and the rushing winds of heaven landed among us!

In more recent times I heard it again. A church full of young people from Scotland were visiting a nearby revival centre where I was preaching. Before I spoke, our host asked the youth group to sing a worship song for us. As the sweet, fresh faced Scots began to sing, I heard again, the sound within the sound. Heaven was in the notes. The fear of God visited that room. Many wept, many others could not move.

Just this year I found myself speaking for a large denomination in Spain, at their annual convention. The larger meetings were good, but quite normal; with passionate, healthy worship and bold preaching. But then I was asked to speak to 200 youth leaders. I shared about intimacy with God and revival for a short while and then we prayed. Once again, without any musical manipulations, something engulfed the group, and through the tears of worship and longing, I once again heard the distinct sound with the sound – the sound of revival, as heaven and humanity fused together for a moment in divine prayer.

I am part of a global network of prophetic creatives called Sounds of the Nations, and our leader and founder, Dan McCollam tells of the time he was involved in leading worship in the 1990's. As the worship leader sang the word "fire" in spontaneous worship and prayer, a sound like a rams horn blasted through the sanctuary from the heavens. Every time the worship leader sang "fire" the supernatural sound would echo – to the amazement of all gathered! I have seen the videos of this event and it is quite remarkable and astonishing, just like Acts chapter 2!

A newspaper headline during the days of the Welsh Revival proclaimed "Something from another world is at work in Wales" – That was over 100 years ago, but the sounds of revival from heaven are still stirring our souls to prepare for the coming glory of the Lord.

The excellent book you hold in your hand is all about this sound from heaven, the supernatural noise of revival, and so much more. Andrew brilliantly joins scripture, prophecy, storytelling and illustration, to raise our faith and sensitivity in order to walk in rhythm with all God is doing in our day.

The sound of revival is being released upon the earth. God is releasing a new rhythm for our era. And those who hear it, those who echo it, those who metaphorically dance to it, will see God's Kingdom come to earth in glory.

By the time the 7th and final trumpet sounds in the heavens, we know that the kingdoms of this world will have become "the kingdoms of our God." (Revelation 11:15) The church will be revived. Society will be transformed. Ultimately all will be renewed. And the earth will be filled with the glory of the Lord, as the waters cover the sea. It is coming – and we must learn to listen for His Sound, that we may walk with God through incredible days of glory.

*Jarrod Cooper*
*Senior leader, Revive Church*
*Jarrod Cooper is an author, songwriter, broadcaster & communicator, and is privileged to lead Revive Church in Hull & East Yorkshire.*

# Introduction

As you study the Scriptures you will often find this principle at work – when God moves, it is accompanied by a sound. Whether it was the sound of Him walking in the Garden of Eden, the sound of an abundance of rain that Elijah heard, the rattling sound in the valley that Ezekiel heard or the sound of a mighty rushing wind on the Day of Pentecost – every new move of heaven comes with a new sound from heaven.

A number of years ago I was ministering in a church and I noticed a lady standing to one side during the worship time. As I saw her, I heard the voice of God speaking a word over her life. Going over to her I told her, "I believe God wants you to know that He loves you". The woman's response was not particularly overwhelming and so I quickly moved away. But then came the sound again. Going over a second time I told her, "God wants you to know that He loves you". The woman's response was even more underwhelming the second time so once again I moved away. But once again, I could the sound of heaven over this woman's life. Going over a third time I told her, "God wants you to know that He loves you". At this, the woman politely smiled and walked out of the building!

I forgot all about this until over a year later when I visited the same church. After the service a lady came over to me and explained that she was the woman who the year before I had told three times that God loved her. She explained that she had been pretty underwhelmed on the night by this seemingly obvious word. However, a short time later this woman found out that her husband had been having an affair and was now leaving her. In her devastation this woman had contemplated suicide. Then she said she had heard my voice "God loves you. God loves you. God loves you". In that moment she realised how loved and valuable she was. In gratitude to God she told how that word had sustained her during this difficult period.

This is what happens when the sound of heaven is spoken over our lives. Daniel found that the sound of God's voice gave him strength as peace and favour was released over his life (Daniel 10:19) whilst Ezekiel found that the sound of God's voice caused him to be raised up as the Spirit filled him (Ezekiel 2:1-2).

Heaven's sound strengthens us, sustains us, empowers us and lifts us to a place of destiny and victory.

Heaven's sound also has a powerful effect upon satan and his demons. In 2 Kings 7, the Arameans, the enemies of God's people, have surrounded Samaria when something remarkable happens:

*"….for the Lord had caused the Arameans to hear the sound of chariots and horses and a great army, so that they said to one another, 'Look, the king of Israel has hired the Hittite and Egyptian kings to attack us!' So, they got up and fled in the dusk and abandoned their tents and their horses and donkeys. They left the camp as it was and ran for their lives." (2 Kings 7:6-7)*

The result of the enemy fleeing was that the people of God were delivered and they ended up plundering the Aramean camp.
Although God's people were surrounded by their enemies, they were surrounded by something more powerful than their enemies. Psalm 32 tells us that God surrounds His people with songs of deliverance (Psalm 32:7). In the natural, Israel was surrounded by the Arameans, but in the spirit realm they were surrounded by heaven's song. It was the sound of heaven that brought confusion to the enemies' plans, caused their army to turn and run and enabled God's people to be liberated and restored.

There is a sound that brings victory. There is a sound that redeems. There is a sound that causes the enemy to panic. There is a sound that releases the provision of God. It is the sound that ends fear, that causes strongholds to break and mountains to move. This is the sound of heaven that protects, covers and surrounds all of God's people. It is both a love song and a battle cry, the sound of the Great Warrior and our heavenly Bridegroom. It invites us in, heals and transforms us and then empowers us to win every fight.

But are we listening? Can we hear the sound of heaven?

John 12 tells us of an occasion in the life of Jesus when God spoke loudly and clearly over His Son:

*"Then a voice came from heaven, 'I have glorified it, and will glorify it again.' The crowd that was there and heard it said it had thundered; others said an angel had spoken to Him." (v28-29)*

As Heaven's sound was released some only heard thunder – they could hear that something was happening but didn't relate it to anything spiritual. Others thought it was an angel – they linked the sound with some kind of supernatural phenomenon. But those who were tuned in recognised that this was the sound of heaven – God was speaking.

I believe we are living in days when God is speaking over the earth like never before. There is a sound of awakening being released over the nations. His voice is shaking economies, governments and political systems. His voice is shaking the media and the entertainment world. His voice is bringing revival to His Church. His voice is bringing clarity and strategy for an end time move of God. His voice is calling home the lost and the prodigals. His voice is commissioning and releasing people. His voice is bringing life and setting the captives free. His voice is bringing with it new faith for signs and wonders and miracles.

How do you respond to what God is doing on the earth right now? Do you dismiss it, thinking nothing is happening of any great significance? It's just thunder, just a noise. Or do you get caught up with the sign, the wonder, the manifestation but miss the greater point? The point is this – God is communicating to His children. Father God is saying to humanity, "Adam, where are you?"

God is longing for relationship, intimacy with you. He longs to speak to you, sing over you and guide and direct you with His words of truth and life.

Many of us have been deaf to what God is wanting to say to us, but I believe we are in a Mark 7 moment:

*"Then Jesus left the vicinity of Tyre and went through Sidon, down to the Sea of Galilee and into the region of the Decapolis. There some people brought to Him a man who was deaf and could hardly talk, and they begged Jesus to place His hand on him.*

*After He took him aside, away from the crowd, Jesus put His fingers into the man's ears. Then He spat and touched the man's tongue. He looked up to heaven and with a deep sigh said to him, 'Ephphatha!' (which means 'Be opened!'). At this, the man's ears were opened, his tongue was loosed, and he began to speak plainly."*
*(Mark 7:31-35)*

In the noisy world that we live in, how easily we become deaf to the sound of our Father's voice. It all begins with Him taking us aside, us getting alone with Him. This is the great need of our day – to shut out every noise and every distraction and just get alone with Jesus. It is in that place that He can touch our spiritual ears and speak "Ephphatha" over us – "be opened!" He longs to open our spiritual ears so that we can hear His voice and know His thoughts and ways.

*Job 37 instructs us: "Hear attentively the noise of His voice, and the sound that goeth out of His mouth" (v2 – KJV).*

Would you join me on the pages of this book as together we learn the need to get alone with Jesus, have Him open our ears so that we can lean in and listen attentively to heaven's sound? It is this sound that will change our world and the world around us.

"Wrong will be right, when Aslan comes in sight. At the sound of his roar, sorrows will be no more. When he bares his teeth, winter meets its death. And when he shakes his mane, we shall have spring again."

*- The Lion, The Witch and The Wardrobe – C.S. Lewis*

# CAN YOU HEAR WHAT I HEAR?

*"Arise, my dearest. Hurry, my darling.*
*Come away with me!*
*I have come as you have asked*
*to draw you to my heart and lead you out.*
*For now is the time, my beautiful one.*

*The season has changed,*
*the bondage of your barren winter has ended,*
*and the season of hiding is over and gone.*
*The rains have soaked the earth*
*and left it bright with blossoming flowers.*

*The season for singing and pruning the vines has arrived.*
*I hear the cooing of doves in our land,*
*filling the air with songs to awaken you*
*and guide you forth.*

*Can you not discern this new day of destiny*
*breaking forth around you?*
*The early signs of my purposes and plans*
*are bursting forth.*

> *The budding vines of new life*
> *are now blooming everywhere.*
> *The fragrance of their flowers whispers,*
> *"There is change in the air."*
>
> *Arise, my love, my beautiful companion,*
> *and run with me to the higher place.*
> *For now is the time to arise and come away with me."*
>
> (Song of Songs 2:8-10) - TPT

What we have here are words from the Song of Solomon, an ancient piece of Hebrew poetry probably written by King Solomon about a king and his lover. Some translators prefer to call this writing the Song of Songs and this is my preferred title, for this is what it is – the song of all songs, the ultimate song, the most powerful of all songs ever written. It is a love song, a song of passion, longing, intimacy and zeal.

Some theologians and scholars see this writing as a celebration of human love between a man and a woman. Others see it as a type or picture of God and Israel. Still others see this book as a picture of Christ and His Church. Although I believe there is truth in all of these interpretations, I believe it is the later that really is the heart of this book. I believe that the Song of Songs is ultimately about the divine romance that Jesus has for His Bride, the Church, and that this love song is what He is singing over us right now.

In chapter two, the bridegroom makes a powerful prophetic statement to his lover.

He simply declares "the season has changed".

The king's lover has evidently been in a season which is described as a "barren winter". The image is one of no life, no fruit, no growth. Nothing is happening, the ground is tough, and everything seems so hard.

The king describes how she feels trapped in this barren winter – she is in bondage, her barrenness is a prison that she can't escape from. No matter what she does or no matter how hard she tries she can't change the circumstances or environment that she is in.

But now the king comes and declares over her: "The season is over and gone… Can you not discern this new day of destiny… There is change in the air."

Can you imagine the excitement and the relief? This declaration brings with it hope and expectancy. The king is bringing her into a new season – one that is full of life, full of fruitfulness, full of joy and full of purpose and destiny.

As believers we must understand that times and seasons belong to God. Daniel 2 says "He (God) changes times and seasons" (v21).

The good news is that this God who changes times and seasons is our loving, Heavenly Father. That means His desire is that we wouldn't live in the barrenness of winter but in the fruitfulness of spring.

He is the God who declares light into darkness; He creates and sustains everything with His powerful word. He is the God whose voice calms storms, moves mountains and raises the dead.

This same God has the power and authority to come to those who feel like they are living in the bondage of winter and declare over them: "The season is over and gone… Can you not discern this new day of destiny… There is change in the air."

These aren't just empty words of wishful thinking – this is the God who "calls into being things that were not" (Romans 4:17). When He declares a new season over your life, you can be certain that His Word has the power to propel us into that which He has spoken.

**A New Season**

I personally believe that God is announcing a new season over His Church. Looking at the Church worldwide, in recent decades there have been great moves of God in Africa, Asia and South America. These have resulted in an incredible harvest of souls.

But it seems like the Church in the West – the USA to some extent and Europe to a greater extent – has been in a barren winter. Although there have been some signs of life and little pockets where God has moved, by and large the Church has struggled to grow. There have been few signs of large numbers of salvations, of prodigals returning an-masse, of the signs and wonders that are supposed to accompany the gospel. Little by little the Church has lost its influence in the nations as society has become more and more secular.

Meanwhile Christians have been working hard, faithfully praying and seeking God, and yet it seems that, no matter how hard we have worked or strived, things just aren't changing.

But I believe that a new season is on the way! I believe that once again God is singing a new song over His Church! I believe we are coming into a new day of the Holy Spirit's outpouring, a new day of visitation, a new day of us seeing God's Kingdom here on earth. You can call it revival, or reformation or outpouring, it doesn't really matter, but I believe we are going to see salvations like never before, prodigals returning like never before, an ease in praying for the sick, signs and wonders becoming common, moves of God's Spirit, churches growing, communities changing, believers returning to their first love, nations turning back to God!

Of course we can talk about grand themes like this and sometimes get lost in the scale of it all, so why don't we make it personal? How about your winter ending? How about your barrenness ceasing? How about you, your marriage, your family, your ministry, your finances entering into a new season? How about you entering into a new day of blessing, of favour, of health, of abundance, of prosperity?

## A New Sound

What is interesting as we read again Song of Songs 2 is that this new season is accompanied by a new sound. The King describes this as "the season of singing" with "the cooing of doves" and "the air filled with the songs of awakening". Even the fragrance of the flowers is whispering a sound.

We of course see this in the natural world. As I write this chapter, we have just entered the season of spring. It seems that there are sounds I have not heard during winter that are suddenly being released again – the sound of children playing outside, the sound of the lawnmower cutting grass, the sound of birds tweeting, the sound of bees buzzing, the sound of new born lambs bleating.

As winter transitions into spring, the new season is accompanied by a new sound.

This is not only true in the natural, but the spiritual too. You often find on the pages of scripture that whenever God does a new thing, along with it comes a new sound.

*"The God of gods, the mighty Lord Himself, has spoken!*
*He shouts out over all the people of the earth*
*in every brilliant sunrise and every beautiful sunset,*
*saying, "Listen to Me!"*
*God's glory-light shines out of the Zion-realm*
*with the radiance of perfect beauty.*

*With the rumble of thunder He approaches;*
*He will not be silent, for He comes with an ear-splitting sound!*
*All around Him are furious flames of fire,*
*and preceding Him is the dazzling blaze of his glory.*

*Here He comes to judge His people!*
*He summons His court with heaven and earth as His jury, saying,*
*"Gather all My lovers, My godly ones whose hearts are one with Me–*
*those who have entered into My holy covenant"*
*(Psalm 50:1-5) – TPT*

Psalm 50 is a powerful description of God coming in power from heaven to earth. Although this can ultimately refer to the second coming of Jesus, I believe prophetically we can see a glimpse into God visiting our churches, our lives, our homes and our communities with His revival power.

When God comes in Psalm 50 He comes with glory and fire! As He comes, He will not be silent. His coming is accompanied by noise – He is speaking, He is shouting, there is the rumble of thunder! There is an ear splitting sound that is a sign that the King is coming! God is on the move!

## The Sound of Glory

The glory of God is one of the major themes in the writings of the prophet Ezekiel. The glory of God can be described as the weight of God's majesty, His splendour, the fullness of His presence. The glory of God is His beauty, His holiness, His Kingdom authority, His power all rolled into one. The glory is His goodness and His goodness is His glory.

In truth it is impossible to adequately describe the glory of God using human words. Some things you just have to experience! All I know is that you were created to know and experience and live in His glory. When His glory turns up, everything changes. Satan cannot stand in the glory of God. Neither can sin, sickness, bondage, fear, shame, unbelief. You will know when you experience His glory. In His glory you are truly changed. You are never the same again.

When Ezekiel talks about the glory of God, he seems to be describing something that is tangible, something that can be experienced but also something that can move. This concept is seen elsewhere in Scripture as Habakkuk declares that one day "the earth will be filled with the knowledge of the glory of the Lord as the waters cover the sea".

Although there is a sense in which the whole earth is already filled with His glory (Isaiah 6), the earth or rather the peoples of the earth don't know that yet! They aren't aware of it, they haven't experienced it. But as the mighty oceans move, the glory of God is on the move: visiting churches, touching lives, reviving His people, transforming nations.

Ezekiel describes the movement of God's glory like this: "Then the Spirit lifted me up, and I heard behind me a loud rumbling sound as the glory of the Lord rose from the place where it was standing" (Ezekiel 3:12).

Notice that as the glory of God moves, it is accompanied by a sound – in this case a loud rumbling sound.

In chapter 43 of Ezekiel there is a powerful moment when the glory of God, which has departed from the temple, returns and once again fills the house of God. Again, this move of God's glory is accompanied by a sound – this time the roar of rushing waters (v2).

Today the temple of God is no longer a building built by man, but the place where God lives and dwells is us, His people, His Church. God's great desire is that we would see His glory (John 17:24) and that His glory would fill His Church (Ephesians 3:21).

I believe we are living in those days when the glory of God is being experienced like never before. And with that glory comes a new sound! It is the sound of awakening, the sound of a new day, the dove (the Holy Spirit) is once again cooing in our land!

## The Sound of the Spirit

> "When the day of Pentecost came, they were all together in one place. Suddenly a sound like the blowing of a violent wind came from heaven and filled the whole house where they were sitting. They saw what seemed to be tongues of fire that separated and came to rest on each of them. All of them were filled with the Holy Spirit and began to speak in other tongues as the Spirit enabled them." (Acts 2:1-4)

In Acts 2, 120 believers are gathered in an upper room waiting for the promise of the Father, the Holy Spirit to be poured out. They had probably been waiting for 10 days before the feast of Pentecost arrived. During that time they had not been sat idly waiting. They had been praying, they had been praising, they had been asking God to send His Spirit.

You can just imagine the sounds that were coming out of the Upper Room. The sounds of petition, sounds of longing, frustration, groaning, tears. Sounds of prayer and singing, sounds of worship all filled the air.

But on the day of Pentecost itself, suddenly there was another sound that entered the room. This sound drowned out the sound of their praying. It was a sound so powerful that it 'filled the house'. Can you imagine a sound so powerful that you can actually feel it? Translators describe it as the sound of a 'rushing mighty wind', 'a violent wind', 'a violent tempest blast', 'the howling of a fierce wind', 'the roar of a violent wind', 'a strong wind blowing', 'a mighty windstorm', 'a strong driving wind', 'a violent breath'.

You get the idea! It was not a physical wind that entered the room, it was a sound that filled the room! A sound so mighty, so strong, so violent, so powerful that the whole house reverberated with the sound. A sound that caused them to feel like the whole building was shaking!

What was the source of this sound? All translators are clear: this was a sound that 'came from heaven'. This was not the sound of the disciples. This was not the sound of the worship team! This was not hype or sensationalism. This was a heavenly sound. A divine sound.

This sound wasn't just noise by itself. This sound was accompanied by something – it was accompanied with fire; it was accompanied by the Holy Spirit Himself.

For the disciples this sound was the sign that everything was about to change. This day was the start of a whole new era of God dealing with man. On this day the Church of Jesus Christ was born. On this day, God Himself came to live in human hearts. On this day ordinary men and women were clothed with the very power of God. This was a new day of closeness, of resurrection life, of transformed hearts. It ushered them into a day of evangelism, of boldness, of signs and wonders. And it was all accompanied by a sound.

In fact it was the case in Acts 2 that the sound preceded the move of the Holy Spirit. Before they saw the fire and felt the Spirit they first heard the sound.

Quite often before we see God at work, we will hear Him. Often there is first the sound and then the manifestation. Many times we will hear the proclamation of the new season before we see the fruit of the new season.

That means that what I can see is less important than what I can hear.

## The Sound of Bells

Exodus 28 describes in some detail the garments that Aaron the high priest would wear as he went into the Holy Place to minister to the Lord. Verse 32 tells us that Aaron would wear gold bells around the hem of his robe. Verse 33 tells us "the sound of the bells will be heard when he enters the Holy Place before the Lord".

I find it interesting that when the high priest went through the veil into the presence of God, the people on the outside couldn't see what he was doing. How did they know that he was at work, doing his priestly ministry? How did they know he wasn't asleep or dead or watching television?! Because there was a sound! There was a sound of bells coming out of the presence of God. As long as they could hear the sound of bells, they knew that the high priest was alive and at work!

For the believer today our High Priest is Jesus Himself. Do you know that Jesus is alive and at work in your life and in your circumstances? Do you know that Jesus is on the move in the nations of the world?

I'll be honest, sometimes I look at my life and wonder – is God really at work? I look at my nation and think – God are you really moving?

Sometimes we look at our circumstances and wonder – is God really there? I certainly can't see Him!

But for a moment, just stop. Stop and pause. Take your eyes off of your circumstances. Take your eyes off of what is happening around you. Stop and listen. Can you hear it? It's the sound of bells! It's the sound that the King is still on the throne. It's the sound that Jesus is still alive and still at work!

The truth is that God often does His best work in the dark where you can't see Him. When Jesus was laid in the grave, it appeared like it was all over. The devil thought that he had won; the religious leaders thought that they had won. Even the disciples thought Jesus had failed.

See the dead body of Jesus lying in darkness, lying in the grave. What can you hear? Nothing? All is quiet? All is silent? Listen a little harder. It may be a faint sound that you can hear but from far far away, in another dimension, if you listen close enough, you can hear the sound of keys! It is the sound of the keys of death and hades being snatched from satan's grip. It is the sound of prison doors being opened. It is the sound of death being defeated. It is the sound of captivity being made captive!

The greatest triumph, the greatest victory, happened when all was dark. Just because you can't see Jesus at work right now, it doesn't mean He isn't at work! Can you hear Him? Can you hear the sound of bells? Can you hear the sound from Heaven? It is the signal – something is coming!

For my family, one of our favourite festive movies is The Polar Express. We usually watch it each Christmas Eve accompanied by some hot chocolate! At the end of the movie, the main character is given a bell from Santa's sleigh. On Christmas morning the boy and his younger sister Sarah are delighted to hear the sweet ringing of the bell as they shake it. However the parents, who no longer believe in Santa, shake the bell and can't hear anything, explaining that it must be broken. The movie ends with the now adult boy lamenting that for his friends and his sister, they gradually grew deaf to the bell as their belief faded over the years. The bell, however, still rings for him, as it will do for all those who truly believe.

For many believers they have heard so many prophetic words of coming moves of God, talk of revival, declarations that this is a new time – and yet it has seemed to come to no fruition. They have stopped truly believing that God could move by His glory again in our day. They seem to have plateaued, believing that the way things are is the way that things will always be.

That have become deaf to the sound of bells.

Other believers have lived in the hardship of winter for so long that they have lost all hope that a new season could be theirs.

They too can no longer hear the sound of bells.

But I believe, whether we are disappointed cynics or burnt out and weary, God is wanting us to recapture a childlike sense of faith and expectancy and believe once again that:

*"I (God) am about to do something….that will make the ears of everyone who hears about it tingle." (1 Samuel 3:11)*


## Your sound must change

A few years ago I was on a mission's trip preaching the gospel in the country of Macedonia. It was one of those beautiful spring evenings in mainland Europe – the kind when you can walk outside in shorts and a T-Shirt when you'd probably be wrapped up warm indoors with a hot drink back in England! Myself and the team with me were walking past the river that runs through the middle of this particular city when we began to hear the sound of music coming from across the other side of the river. It was the sound of a band playing live instrumental music.

I paused for a moment, certain that I recognised the song that was being played but temporarily being unable to place it. Then it dawned on me – the song that they were playing was a Christmas carol! For a moment I was in a daze and I turned to the team to confirm that what I was hearing was correct. A Christmas carol – but in the middle of spring. A good song, a great song – but the wrong season!

I felt like going over to the band and asking them, "Hasn't anyone told you that the season has changed? This isn't the right sound for this season!"

I felt the Holy Spirit whisper into my heart, "This is my Church. I am trying to bring them into spring but they are still singing the songs of winter".

I firmly believe that as the Church we are not to just sit around and wait for God to do something, hoping that one day things will change. I believe today is the day of salvation. Today His Kingdom is at hand. Today His power and glory are available. I don't need to live in winter or barrenness another moment – He changed my season and He changed it forever when He died and rose again. I should never live in death or decay but always live in the fruit of the finished work of Jesus on the cross.

But I also believe that my sound determines my season. Indeed the sound that my life produces will either keep me trapped in a permanent winter or propel me into a glorious spring.

Not only must I hear the new sound from Heaven but, if I want to see the fruit of that, then that new sound has to be on my lips also.

The old sounds of unbelief, of cynicism, of religiosity have to be banished from our lives.

The sounds of winter have no place in what God is wanting to do now.

> "He put a new song in my mouth, a hymn of praise to our God." (Psalm 40)

It is time to declare a new sound – a sound of hope, of faith, of excitement, of expectancy.

> "Yahweh your God is there with you, the warrior-Saviour. He will rejoice over you with happy song, He will renew you by His love, He will dance with shouts of joy for you." (Zephaniah 3:17) – NJB

According to Zephaniah God right now is making a sound over your life! Right now He is singing over your circumstances, over your church, over your nation.

The sound that Heaven is producing over you is a happy sound! It is a sound of joy, a sound of love, a sound of triumph, a sound of freedom and a sound of victory!

The invitation from Holy Spirit is to lean in and listen to that sound.

The challenge of the Holy Spirit is to take that sound and let it be your sound, your song and your confession.

**Releasing heaven's sound**

The book of Revelation was originally a letter written by the Apostle John to seven churches in the region of Asia Minor. From chapter 1, verse 9 onwards, John describes his vision of the glorified Jesus, the throne-room of heaven and various apocalyptic events including the second coming of Christ. So, if chapter 1, verse 9 onwards is the description of John's revelation, the first 8 verses are the introduction, written after the event, setting the scene for what is to come.

Why is that significant? Because in verse 4, (remember this is written after John has had his encounter) he uses this title of Jesus "Him who is, and who was, and who is to come". There are many words used in the book of Revelation that are directly referencing themes and images used elsewhere in Scripture, but this title that John uses, "Him who is, and who was, and who is to come" is unique to John and to this book.

So, where did John get the idea that Jesus is the One who is, and was, and who is to come?

Well in chapter 4, John is caught up into the throne room of heaven and sees an incredible vision of God seated on the throne, surrounded by angelic worship. In the presence of God, John can hear a sound, it is the sound of living creatures singing to God. And what are the words of their praise:

*"'Holy, holy, holy is the Lord God Almighty," who was, and is, and is to come." (v8)*

It was in the presence of God, in the throne room of heaven that John heard the sound filling the atmosphere, declaring that Jesus is the One who was, is and is to come.

What does John do with heaven's sound? He then takes that sound and releases on the earth in his letters to the Church. When he describes Jesus in chapter 1, he is not coming up with some original thought or something that he has made up himself. He is releasing the sound that he has first heard in heaven.

This is my great desire in writing this book. Understand that heaven is making a sound over your life, over your church, over your community and over your nation. Heaven is declaring who Jesus is and who you are in Him. Heaven is singing a love song, a song pregnant with hope and purpose over your church, over your circumstances, over your town and city.

God is looking for a people that know what it is to be "in the Spirit" (1:10) and to respond to the call to be caught up into His presence and before His throne lean in and listen. What is heaven saying? What are the words and the sounds and the songs that are coming from the throne room? Your job and my job, is to then take those sounds and release them on the earth – through prayer, prophesy, declaration, worship, action – we take what heaven is saying and singing and doing and then we release it on the earth.

*"He who sent me is trustworthy, and what I have heard from Him I tell the world (John 8:26)*

Jesus knew what it was to hear and then to release what He had heard. It was this partnership with heaven that brought God's Kingdom to earth and saw lives transformed wherever He went. This too is our mandate, this is the invitation we all have – to turn winter into spring, to bring heaven to earth. But it all starts by leaning in and listening. Can you hear what I hear?

# LISTENING TO THE SOUND

*"As Jesus and His disciples were on their way, He came to a village where a woman named Martha opened her home to Him. She had a sister called Mary, who sat at the Lord's feet listening to what He said. But Martha was distracted by all the preparations that had to be made. She came to Him and asked, 'Lord, don't you care that my sister has left me to do the work by myself? Tell her to help me!' 'Martha, Martha,' the Lord answered, 'you are worried and upset about many things, but few things are needed – or indeed only one. Mary has chosen what is better, and it will not be taken away from her." (Luke 10:38-42)*

One of the titles of Jesus is the "Word". Jesus is God's Word, the Living Word, God's revelation. Jesus doesn't just speak God's words, He is God's Word. When Martha opened up her home to Jesus she was opening up a world of possibility. In opening up her home to Jesus, Martha was giving herself a unique opportunity to hear the sound of heaven – the sound of God Himself.

What a vital thing it is to open up our homes, our lives and our spirits to hear the sound of heaven. Martha was inviting the One whose words brought creation into existence into her home. She was inviting the One whose words sustain all things. Creation responded to His sound. The wind and the waves obeyed that sound. Sickness departed at the sound of His voice. Demons fled at the sound of His command. Even death itself gave up its prisoners at the sound of His word.

In inviting the Word into her home, Martha was inviting in the One whose sound could bring life, health, healing, the impossible, creative miracles right into her world! What an opportunity.

And yet tragically Martha failed to take advantage of this incredible opportunity. Martha probably had every intention of listening to the sound of Jesus' voice and yet she found herself being pulled away by all the distractions of the things that had to be done.

As believers we too have the incredible opportunity to commune with the Living Word. When we receive the sound of heaven we are receiving the most powerful, life-giving, life-creating, life-sustaining force in the universe. When the power and truth and sound of His voice fills our homes, our families and our lives we are opening up a world of unlimited potential.

How many of us have every desire for Jesus to speak into our lives? "God speak to me!" "God, I want to know You." "God, I long for deeper friendship with You." Like Martha we pray prayers that invite Him in. Our intentions are good. But then comes the pull of distractions. The pull of work. The pull of television. The pull of social media. The pull of seemingly important commitments. And in responding to that pull we fail to take advantage of all that is available just by stopping and listening.

The distractions may seem legitimate, but if they take us away from listening to His sound then they are an enemy of our peace and joy. Worry, upset, frustration – these were the results of Martha responding to the pull away from Jesus and towards the work and preparations that seemingly had to be made.
But there is another pull. This is the pull that Mary responded to. It is the pull to ignore the distractions and listen to the sound of His voice. Notice that Mary "chose" to do this. She chose to sit at His feet and listen. Jesus will very rarely hit you over

the head with His Word. Instead He invites you into a place where you can listen. Do you respond to that call?

It's an invitation to sit. To be seated is a posture of rest. It means that Mary ceased from her activities. She gave Jesus her undivided attention. It was a posture of focus and devotion. Her one priority was to listen to the sound of heaven - the sound of the voice of Jesus.

Two sisters. Both had the same opportunity to hear His voice, yet one responded to the distractions and the other responded to the invitation to sit and listen to the sound of heaven.

Jesus said that Mary had chosen that which was "better". The Greek word "better" is the word "agathos". It means that which is good, profitable, useful, beneficial, advantageous - inherent goodness. This is the power of listening to His voice.

Ceasing from activity, stopping, sitting, listening to His voice - it is never a waste of time. Listening to the sound of heaven is to our advantage. It is of benefit to us. We are filling our lives with that which is good and profitable.

The book of Amos speaks of a day when there would be a famine in the land. A famine of "hearing the words of the Lord" (Amos 8:11). Notice that it would not be a famine of the words of the Lord - it would not be a case of God not speaking. It would be case of people not hearing, not listening to this sound.

Could it be that this famine came about because people were no longer taking the time to stop, sit and listen to the One whose words give life?

The voice of God is described in Revelation 1:15 as "the sound of rushing waters"

– in other words there is a continual flow. The sound of heaven is not like a tap that can be turned on or off. He is not speaking one minute and then silent the next. He never stops speaking. His voice is a continual sound of life and power. He never stops communicating with us.

But we have become deaf because we have become too busy. Too distracted. We have lost our focus.

Every day we must fight against the pull of distractions and make hearing His voice our one thing, our priority, our greatest prize and our greatest goal.

**Created to hear**

John 8:47 contains a wonderful promise from Jesus:

*"Whoever belongs to God hears what God says. The reason you do not hear is that you do not belong to God."*

Do you "belong" to God? Does He own you, possess you? Is He the One you have made Lord? The promise is, that the sign of His ownership over you is that you now have the ability to hear His voice, His sound. This is your right as a child of God. This is the honour and privilege of God's children. It is a promise from Jesus that you can hear the voice of your Father.

It is now our responsibility to take hold of this wonderful promise and to position our lives so that we can hear. In the same way that if I pray the prayer of faith I can expect healing, and if I sow I can expect to reap, if I learn to push distractions to one side and sit at the feet of Jesus, I can expect to hear the sound of His voice.

In speaking of the Holy Spirit, Jesus said in John 16, that when He comes "He will speak". The Holy Spirit is not a force, a feeling or a sensation. He is a person. When He comes into our lives, He comes to communicate heaven's sound.

Jesus said, "He will not speak on His own, He will speak only what He hears". When I am preaching overseas I will often have a translator. A good translator will not preach his own sermon! He will speak only what he hears. A good translator will listen to what I am saying and communicate those words, even the tones and the feelings behind the words in a way that the people can understand.

The Holy Spirit is God's translator. Right now the Holy Spirit is listening to the sounds of the throne room. He is listening to what Father and Jesus are speaking, singing and declaring over your life, your circumstances and your world. Holy Spirit then takes those sounds and speaks them directly into your spirit in a way that you can understand. This is why we all hear God in different ways but the source is the same – the throne room, and the communicator is the same – the Holy Spirit.

## My sheep know My voice

In John 10, Jesus gives us some wonderful insights into His voice and the sound of heaven.

> "The gatekeeper opens the gate for him, and the sheep listen to his voice. He calls his own sheep by name and leads them out. When he has brought out all his own, he goes on ahead of them, and his sheep follow him because they know his voice. But they will never follow a stranger; in fact, they will run away from him because they do not recognise a stranger's voice." (v3-5)

Again, how do you know that you belong to Him? You listen to His voice. You take time to push away distractions, you respond to the invitation to sit at His feet, and you stop and you pause and you listen.

It is in the listening that you come to recognise His voice. In the days of cell phones this illustration may no longer be relevant, but for those who still use a landline occasionally you may answer and the person on the other end, rather than giving their name, will simply say "it's me". They presume that you will know who they are just by the sound of the voice. They are assuming a level of relationship. They are assuming that they are not a stranger to you.

Have you ever had the awkward moment of someone saying "it's me" and you don't have a clue who they are? Hopefully that was never with your spouse or a parent or a close friend or colleague! To be unsure of whose voice it is would be a clear sign that you don't know them as well as you should. But someone you know, someone you are familiar with, someone in whose presence you spend a lot of time, someone who you listen to on a regular basis, they only have to say "it's me" and you know immediately who it is.

Someone who truly knows God, doesn't need a visit from an angel, 15 confirmations or a hand to write on the wall to know that God is speaking. Someone who knows what it is to sit at His feet and listen only needs the faintest of promptings and you know, you just know – that is my Jesus speaking. I have become used to His sound, I have become familiar with what His voice sounds like.

It is interesting that Jesus said that the sheep know His "voice". The implication is that they don't just hear His words, but that it is the sound that they recognise. Sheep of course don't understand or comprehend words or their meaning, but they do recognise the "sound" of the shepherd's voice.

Just hearing the words of Jesus is not enough. The shepherd and the stranger can both say the exact same word to the sheep, but one will attract and one will repel the sheep. The difference is not the words themselves but the sound. The shepherd leads to safety, the stranger leads to danger. The key is not in the words but discerning the sound of the voice.

I love the Bible but just hearing His words is not the same as listening to His voice. You can have perfect theology and not know the shepherd. The Pharisees and teachers of the law knew God's word, but they had become deaf to the sound of His voice. Satan can quote the word of God. Some cults or heretical teachers can take God's word and speak it – but the sound is wrong. It is not the sound of His voice.

We have to be people that don't just know His written word but we know His sound – we know what the Shepherd sounds like, we know His voice when He calls us.

*"Lord, if it's you,' Peter replied, 'tell me to come to you on the water.' 'Come,' He said. Then Peter got down out of the boat, walked on the water and came towards Jesus."*
*(Matthew 14:28-29)*

Anyone could have said "come", but Peter knew the sound of His voice. Peter didn't respond to the word itself, but the voice communicating that word. Anyone can preach a sermon, anyone can give good advice, anyone can give us a prophetic word – but those of us listening, we are not just listening to the content. We are listening to the sound. Is that the sound of a man or is that the sound of my Jesus?

The moment Peter knew "that sounds like Jesus", he responded. Likewise, obedience should be our natural response to His voice.

*"His sheep follow him because they know his voice"* (John 10:4)

In the Middle East a shepherd guides his sheep, not by coming behind them and driving them but by walking ahead of them and calling them. As the sheep listen to his voice, they follow the sound of the shepherd as he leads them to good pasture.

Our ability to be led is determined by our ability to firstly listen, but then secondly to follow the sound of His voice. God will not force us into our destiny or the good things He has for us – He will call us into them. Our ability to respond and to obey His voice determines whether we will end up where He wants us and with all that He has for us.

I have learned that each time I obey the sound of His voice, I am propelled into a greater level of intimacy which means I get to hear His voice with greater clarity.

The very first time I gave a prophetic word was in a Tuesday evening prayer meeting at my church. I was a teenager at the time. As we all sat with our heads bowed the pastor asked if anyone felt like they had anything from God. I suddenly felt a prompting in my heart. Looking back the word was so simple and basic. It was just "The Lord is your Shepherd" – straight from scripture. Being unfamiliar to the voice of God, my first reaction was "I'm making it up!" but as I tried to silence this voice, this impression grew stronger and stronger.

As I tried to supress it, other feelings fought against that voice – what if it is the devil? What if I start to speak and everyone laughs at me? What if the pastor rebukes me? But I couldn't fight this feeling that God was speaking.

Eventually, after what seemed like an eternity I stood up and said "God says 'I am your Shepherd'". Then I sat down with my head in my hands overcome by embarrassment. As the meeting ended and people began to leave I stayed sat with my head in my hands wishing the ground would swallow me up. I was certain that I had made a fool of myself.

One of the last people to leave the meeting was a much older lady and as she walked passed me she paused just for a moment. She tapped me on the shoulder and quietly said, "That word was for me" and then she kept walking. Immediately I felt like a weight had been lifted and relief flooded my entire being! I had been right! I had heard from God! I had been right to obey the promptings and release the word.

Now I want to fast forward to a few years later and I am ministering in a prison in Kenya. It was a slightly daunting place with guards who had machine guns and prisoners wearing black and white striped uniforms. I shared a few words before my pastor preached the gospel and several of the men gave their lives to Jesus. At the end of the message, the Kenyan pastor who had arranged the visit announced that we were to go and lay hands on the men who had responded. A little reluctantly I moved among these criminals and started to pray for each one. When I got to one man, I paused. The Holy Spirit had given me a word for him. "Sir", I said, "God has brought you to this prison because He wanted to meet with you here. But very soon you will be released from this prison and when you are on the outside you will serve God". As I gave the word a few people around me began to laugh.

Afterwards they told me what was so funny. The man was in prison for murder. He was under a life sentence. "In our country life means life. This man will never be released. He will die in this prison."

A few weeks later I received an email from the pastor in Kenya. It seemed that there had been a problem in that prison with overcrowding. The government had never before done this in their history, but they had produced a list of prisoners who were in that jail for minor offences and had pardoned them to make room for more serious felons. For some reason that no one could explain, that man's name was on the list! His sentence cancelled. He walked through the doors a free man, upon which he contacted the pastor to tell him the news and dedicate his life to serve God.

I have often shared this second story in churches around the world. It is certainly a more impressive story than the first. The first prophetic word was just repeating a fairly simple Bible verse. The second word was so revelatory and accurate and a literally destiny-changing word for this man. The first was very general but the second was very direct. And yet I know that without the first testimony there wouldn't have been the second testimony. If I had never obeyed the simple voice of God, I would never have been able to receive the more direct and accurate word.

Our ability to hear clearly a new word from heaven is linked with our ability to obey the last word from heaven. People who we recognise as having a powerful prophetic ministry, releasing incredibly accurate and direct words from God, didn't start like that. They started by hearing God's voice in general, vague ways, but they obeyed what He was saying. The more they obeyed, the more His voice became clearer and more direct.

Sometimes we ignore what God is saying or we supress it or we fail to hear it because of the distractions or we simply dismiss it because we don't want to do what He is saying or we don't understand or we are afraid or it seems to be too simple… There are a myriad of reasons why we may fail to respond to His voice. What are the consequences? Next time it becomes just a little bit harder to hear what He is saying. We become more and more dull to His voice until we become deaf to Him and we can no longer hear Him at all.

Obedience is always the key to either becoming more and more dull or more and more sharp prophetically. Disobedience takes us into a prophetic dullness but obedience takes us into realms of hearing His voice with such clarity and accuracy.

Don't be discouraged if you don't think you hear God in incredibly detailed or complex ways. Just listen to the simplicity of what He is telling you and, even if you aren't certain, just respond and obey those promptings. I promise you that each time you obey, the next time you will hear His voice with even greater clarity and even greater accuracy.

## **The sound of thunder**

So what does God sound like? The Bible uses several metaphors to describe what the voice of God sounds like.

One of the most common metaphors to describe the voice of God is thunder:

*"The Lord thundered from heaven; the voice of the Most High resounded"*
*(Psalm 18:13)*

*"To Him who rides across the highest heavens, the ancient heavens, who thunders with mighty voice" (Psalm 68:3)*

The Bible is not saying that God's voice is literal thunder. It is using metaphors that we can understand to show us something that we couldn't possibly understand because it's so mind-blowing – God communicating with us! The Psalmist is saying, 'You want to know what God sounds like? – He sounds like thunder!'

Psalm 29 continues this imagery in even greater detail:

*"The voice of the Lord is over the waters; the God of glory thunders, the Lord thunders over the mighty waters. The voice of the Lord is powerful; the voice of the Lord is majestic. The voice of the Lord breaks the cedars; the Lord breaks in pieces the cedars of Lebanon. He makes Lebanon leap like a calf, Sirion like a young wild ox. The voice of the Lord strikes with flashes of lightning. The voice of the Lord shakes the desert; the Lord shakes the Desert of Kadesh. The voice of the Lord twists the oaks and strips the forests bare. And in His temple all cry, 'Glory!'" (v3-9)*

The Psalmist declares that God's voice is over the waters and the trees. Waters and trees are of course aspects of nature but prophetically they can also be pictures of nations and people. Creation, nations, people – God is speaking and singing and declaring over it all.

The sound of His voice is like thunder. The image here is that His voice is powerful, majestic and awesome.

The cedars of Lebanon were the strongest most powerful trees and yet the sound of His voice causes them to "break". The Hebrew word for "break" is "sabar" which means to crush, to smash, to destroy.

It is clear that when heaven speaks – nothing can stand against that sound. Even Sirion (another name for Mount Hermon) skips at the sound of His voice. When He speaks, that which is seemingly immovable moves like a baby animal.

This is how powerful His voice is! Creation responds to that sound. The idea of creation responding to the thunder of His voice is also seen in the book of Job:

*"Listen! Listen to the roar of His voice, to the rumbling that comes from His mouth"*
*(Job 37:2)*

*"God's voice thunders in marvellous ways; He does great things beyond our understanding! He says to the snow, "Fall on the earth," and to the rain shower, "Be a mighty downpour." (Job 37:5-6)*

Take a moment and read Job 37 out of the Message translation. Be stuck by the majesty and the power of His voice and how creation has to respond to the authority in that voice.

*"Whenever this happens, my heart stops–*
*I'm stunned, I can't catch my breath.*
*Listen to it! Listen to His thunder,*
*the rolling, rumbling thunder of His voice.*

*He lets loose his lightenings from horizon to horizon,*
*lighting up the earth from pole to pole.*
*In their wake, the thunder echoes His voice,*
*powerful and majestic.*

*He lets out all the stops, He holds nothing back.*
*No one can mistake that voice–*
*His word thundering so wondrously,*
*His mighty acts staggering our understanding.*

*He orders the snow, 'Blanket the earth!'*
*and the rain, 'Soak the whole countryside!'*

*No one can escape the weather—it's there.
And no one can escape from God.*

*Wild animals take shelter,
crawling into their dens,
When blizzards roar out of the north
and freezing rain crusts the land.
It's God's breath that forms the ice,
it's God's breath that turns lakes and rivers solid.*

*And yes, it's God who fills clouds with rainwater
and hurls lightning from them every which way.*

*He puts them through their paces—first this way, then that—
commands them to do what he says all over the world.*

*Whether for discipline or grace or extravagant love,
He makes sure they make their mark."*

We see this in the life of Jesus. Sickness responded to the sound of His voice. Demons responded to the sound of His voice. Fish responded to the sound of His voice. A fig tree withered. The wind and the waves were silenced. Even death itself responded to the sound of His voice. His voice is like thunder - it is powerful and majestic and all that hear it respond.

Do we see how powerful it is when we position our lives to hear the sound of His voice? When He speaks, everything that is immovable is moved. His voice like thunder echoes in our bodies, our minds and our souls - sickness has to respond, fear has to respond. Depression, anxiety, shame, addiction - all of these things go as the sound of His voice thunders in our innermost being. This is why sitting at His feet and listening to His voice has to be our priority. Only His voice shifts and changes things.

"The voice of the Lord shakes the desert." (v8) The word "shakes" here is the Hebrew word "hiyl" and it means "to turn in a circle" or it can also mean "to writhe in pain, like the pain of childbirth".

How powerful this is! There is a picture of a desert – a dry, dead, barren wasteland. Then over this barrenness comes the voice of God like thunder! Suddenly things begin to turn and change and transformation begins to come. In the barrenness new things begin to get birthed, life begins to grow where there had once been nothing.

This is the power of His voice! When His voice like thunder comes into our lives, everything begins to change! His voice shakes the dry areas, the dead areas, the barren areas – whether that be our finances, our ministries, our relationships. His voice of thunder shakes things, but with the shaking comes life – new fruit, growth, abundance and transformation! There is no situation that His voice cannot speak into. There is no situation that His voice cannot change.

## The whisper and the waters

Although the idea of God's voice sounding like thunder is throughout scripture, it is not the only metaphor used to describe the sound of His voice.

In a total contrast to the power and the aggression of thunder, in 1 Kings 19 God chooses not to communicate to the prophet Elijah like thunder or in other dramatic ways – winds, earthquakes, fire. Instead when God speaks to Elijah His voice sounds like a gentle whisper (v12).

This is the beauty of God. His voice is unique to each person and unique in each circumstance. Elijah is on the run from Jezebel. He is frightened for his life. He is depressed, exhausted and suicidal. If God had spoken to him like thunder it would have been too much for him to handle.

But God knew this. So He chooses to speak to Elijah in a gentle whisper – God was communicating His grace, His kindness, His tenderness and His comfort.

This is what God does – He communicates not only what we need to hear, but how we need to hear it in each circumstance. God is so good! The same Holy Spirit who comes like a mighty rushing wind and flames of fire is also our Comforter. The same voice that sounds like thunder can also communicate as a gentle whisper.

There are times when we need His voice to come like thunder – to shake, to move, to transform, to shift. There are also times when we need a gentle whisper, revealing His kindness and tenderness.

We don't always know which we need, but He does! There are times I want the whisper but I need the thunder! There are times I want the thunder but need the whisper! He decides, not me!

All I have to do is position myself at His feet and listen, pushing aside every distraction, listening and then acting in obedience to His voice.

One final metaphor we will briefly mention as to what His voice sounds like:

> "His voice was like the sound of rushing waters." (Revelation 1:15)

Water in the Bible always speaks of life, of refreshing, of renewal. Whether His voice is like thunder or a whisper, it is always like rushing waters – it is always life giving, life creating and life sustaining. His voice revives, refreshes and restores. His voice is an absolute necessity. His voice gives life because His voice is life!

> *"Mary sat down attentively before the Master, absorbing every revelation He shared." (Luke 10:39 – TPT)*

Mary sat at the feet of Jesus, her spirit opened and she drank in the words of Jesus like a thirsty person drinks a glass of ice cold water on a hot day. The words of living water became revelations she absorbed and drank from.

Are you thirsty? Then sit at His feet and listen. Drink in the sound of His voice. Let His voice change, transform, shake and shift. Let His voice lead and guide. Let His voice give you life.

# THE SOUND OF INVITATION

*"Deep calls to deep in the roar of Your waterfalls, all Your waves and breakers have swept over me." (Psalm 42:7)*

The meeting was over for everyone else but not for me. As my friends and I sat around in our static caravan, I could hear a sound coming from deep within my spirit. I was a teenager and attending the national conference of the denomination that I was a part of. We had had a powerful evening service with great praise and worship and an inspiring message on prayer. As the speaker had concluded he had invited those who wanted to deepen their prayer life to the front to respond. I had not been able to make it to the front, such was the huge response, but I stood somewhere in the middle of thousands of people that said that they were hungry for God.

But now here we all were sat in our accommodation, just moments after the meeting had ended and it seemed like everyone had forgotten all about it. People were talking about what they wanted to eat, others wanted to know what was on television, and others were talking about sport. I just sat, distressed but unsure why. "Is this what it is all about? Do we attend church, meet with God, but then forget it all and go back to normal the moment the service is over? Is this really all there is?" I tried to dismiss these thoughts. Was I being too heavenly minded? Was I being too judgemental? Surely we can't live on the mountain top all the time, can we? Surely

God wants us to have fun sometimes?

But I couldn't escape the sound. Or rather two sounds. Two sounds deep within my innermost being. One sound was the sound of heaven. It was a sound pulling me deeper. A sound that seemed to being saying, "There is more available". It was a sound inviting me into a place of intimate communion with God. If I were to put words to this sound it seemed like God was saying, "You can know Me if you want. You can have a face to face encounter with Me that will change everything".

The second sound was also coming from deep within me. It was the sound of my spirit. It was an inaudible, inexpressible prayer. A longing. A groaning. "God I want to know You". Was heaven's sound responding to my longing? Or was it the other way round?

While everyone around me was talking, and music was playing, and the television was blasting out, these two sounds drowned out every other sound. I had to meet with God!

I got up and walked out of the place where we were staying and started to run. Where to I had no idea. I just couldn't escape that sound. I had to find somewhere to meet with God. I eventually found a children's play area and sat on one of the swings looking up at the starry sky. All around me was quiet, but the sounds had never been louder. Heaven crying "You can know Me if you want" and my spirit crying "God I want You!"

## The sound from the garden

Even now as I am writing this, I can hear these two sounds coming from a mysterious place deep within the part of me that the Bible calls my 'spirit'. I can hear heaven pulling me, drawing me, inviting me into a place of communion with God. I can hear my spirit crying "Yes Lord" to that invitation – my spirit longing for intimacy, with God, knowing that this is where it gets its oxygen, its breath, its life from.

Right at the beginning, in the Garden, we read of Adam and Eve. In the garden they worked, they ruled, they reigned, they produced fruit.

And yet there was a time when they would hear a sound. The Bible describes this sound as "the sound of the Lord God as He was walking in the garden" (Genesis 3:8). What exactly was it that Adam and Eve heard? Did they hear footsteps? Did they hear a rustling in the trees? Did they hear the sound of a wind blowing? We don't know. But they knew what that sound meant. The sound indicated that it was the time to stop their work, lay down whatever it was that they were doing. It was time to meet with God. The sound of God walking in the garden was an invitation – walk with Him, talk with Him, be with Him.

Have you ever wondered what Adam's prayer life was like? He was in paradise so he didn't have any prayer requests! He had never sinned so he had nothing to repent of? Let's be honest, if we took petition and repentance out of most of our prayer lives there wouldn't be much left! But for Adam, prayer was literally walking with God. It was friendship. Relationship. Intimacy. This is what man was created for.

Still God walks in the cool of the day. Still He enters the garden of our spirits. Still He longs for intimacy with us. Still He is inviting us to lay down whatever it is we are doing and walk with Him. Be with Him. Commune with Him. Be one with Him. Can you hear the sound? Can you hear the sound of Him walking? Can you hear the sound of invitation? Can you the sound calling you deeper?

## The sound from the mountain

In Exodus 19 Israel is camped at the foot of Mount Sinai. As all of the people gather at the foot of the mountain, God tells Moses that something extraordinary is about to happen.

> "I am going to come to you in a dense cloud." (Exodus 19:9)

God is once again going to come and meet with His people. Just like He came into the garden, He is going to come down upon the mountain – but with the same purpose – to meet with His people. To communicate with them. To enable them to be in His presence.

God is very clear to Moses that the people cannot come up the mountain straight away. In fact He instructs Moses to put limits around the mountain and that if anyone breaks through and tries to get up the mountain then they will be put to death (v12).

Why you may wonder? Did God not want to meet with His people? Was He tempting them saying, "Here is My presence, but you can't experience it?"

No. They could come up the mountain. But only when there was a sound!

> "Only when the ram's horn sounds a long blast may they go up the mountain." (v13)

His presence would be accompanied by a sound. His presence is always accompanied by a sound. When they heard that sound, this was their invitation, their signal – it was time to meet with God.

Can you hear the sound of the Lord walking in the garden? Can you hear the sound of the ram's horn? Different sounds, but the same invitation: God saying, "You can meet with Me if you want!"

The Bible describes what happened next.

> *"On the morning of the third day there was thunder and lightning, with a thick cloud over the mountain, and a very loud trumpet blast. Everyone in the camp trembled. Then Moses led the people out of the camp to meet with God, and they stood at the foot of the mountain. Mount Sinai was covered with smoke, because the Lord descended on it in fire. The smoke billowed up from it like smoke from a furnace, and the whole mountain trembled violently. As the sound of the trumpet grew louder and louder, Moses spoke and the voice of God answered him." (Exodus 19:16-19)*

What an awesome sound! The rumbling of thunder. The crack of lightning. And then the blast of the trumpet. Who was playing the trumpet? Not Moses. Not any of the Israelites. Was it an angel standing in the presence of God and blasting the trumpet so that the people could hear? The trumpet got louder and louder and louder. So loud that the mountain began to shake.

This trumpet was signalling: "You can break through the barriers and enter My presence. Respond to that sound. Come up and enter in. You can see Me. You can know Me. You can hear My voice"

But how did the people of Israel respond?

*"When the people saw the thunder and lightning and heard the trumpet and saw the mountain in smoke, they trembled with fear. They stayed at a distance and said to Moses, 'Speak to us yourself and we will listen. But do not let God speak to us or we will die." (Exodus 20:18-19)*

What a terrible moment. Just like Adam and Eve when they heard the sound of heaven, they ran away in fear, afraid of judgement or punishment.

They didn't know that the sound of heaven, as awesome as it was, was not God coming to punish but coming to commune with them.

Then comes this incredible contrast:

*"The people remained at a distance, while Moses approached the thick darkness where God was." (Exodus 20:21)*

Both Moses and the people heard the same sound. But the response was very different. The people stood at a distance and watched. They observed. They never entered in. They didn't understand the purpose of the sound.

But Moses did. He would not stand back and observe the glory. He entered the glory. He wanted to be where God was. He wanted to be in the presence. He wanted to meet with God.

This is why Israel knew the deeds of God, but Moses knew the ways of God (Psalm 103:7) There was a friendship with God that Moses had that was special and unique. He knew God's heart, He knew God's voice, He met with God face to face.

Tragically, this relationship didn't have to be unique. It was available to all. But the majority failed to hear the sound of heaven and respond to the invitation to intimacy.

Sadly today our churches can be full of people who know God's deeds but they don't know God. They know Church. They know theology. They know doctrine. They know songs and sermons. They know about God. But they don't know Him. They have never entered the cloud. They have never seen His face. They have never heard His whisper. They have never felt His kiss. They don't know Him. They don't know His presence. They don't know His glory.

Why? They have failed to respond to heaven's sound.

Our churches have too many like Israel – those who watch and observe. We have too few like Moses – too few who will actually enter into the presence of God and meet with Him.

When you don't actually know God, you end up making a god in your own image. A god who fits in with your culture and your lifestyle. A god that you want and not a God that you need.

This is what Israel did, they made a golden calf. Interestingly as they sacrificed to the golden calf they made a great noise, a noise so great that Moses and Joshua could hear it from up the mountain (Exodus 32). Isn't it interesting that they associated the presence of God with a sound?

But when Moses and Joshua head this sound they didn't recognise it. They discussed among themselves – "Is it the sound of war? The sound of victory? The sound of defeat". They can't place the sound. Eventually Moses recognises the sound of singing.

Because Moses and Joshua had been up the mountain, they knew heavens sound. Because Israel had been at a distance the sound that they made was a cheap replica, an imitation of the real thing. Moses and Joshua just didn't recognise it.

One of the results of the Church not truly knowing God is that our gatherings have a lot of noise, a lot of sound, a lot of singing – but it is not the sound of heaven – it is man's imitation. Tragically many of us don't recognise the difference.

But when you have been up the mountain. When you have been in the presence of the Lord, when you have heard the sound of His voice, the sound of angels, the sound of glory, that is the only sound that will suffice. Nothing else will satisfy.

> "Away with the noise of your songs! I will not listen to the music of your harps."
> (Amos 5:23)

Only those who have heard heaven's sound can make heaven's sound. And there is only one way to hear that sound – to enter in and be in His presence. To know Him. To be His friend.

## Friendship with God

It may surprise you to learn that the first person called a 'prophet' in the Bible is

Abraham (Genesis 20:7). Remarkably you never read of Abraham predicting the future or moving in signs and wonders. There is no book of Abraham containing prophetic oracles. So why does God call this man a prophet?

What do we know of Abraham? Abraham was the friend of God (2 Chronicles 20:7). This is the key. Friendship with God is the foundation of the prophetic. If we ever want to hear the voice of God with clarity and accuracy and then release that sound to others, it begins by being His friend, responding to that invitation to intimacy and knowing what it is to walk with God.

Like Abraham, Moses is also known as the friend of God. Exodus 33 describes how Moses would pitch his tent, some distance away from the camp. This tent was known as 'the tent of meeting' and in it:

*"The Lord would speak to Moses face to face, as one speaks to a friend." (v11)*

If we truly want to know God then we must learn to "pitch our tent". We must know what it is to build a tent of meeting in our lives. We must have a place away from the camp – away from distractions, from other people, from social media, from all the tasks that need to be done – just a place where we can meet with God.

God so longs to meet with us 'face to face', literally meaning 'presence to presence'. It is in this place, spirit to spirit, where our hearts are naked and unguarded before Him, that we develop friendship and intimacy.

Notice, that the Bible doesn't say that Moses spoke to God but that God spoke to Moses. There are times when we need to refrain from speaking and just listen to the sound of His voice.

John the Baptist used a beautiful phrase to describe himself in John 3. John said that he was 'the friend of the bridegroom' (v29). I find this one of the most moving descriptions of a relationship with Jesus in the scriptures.

Although John was a mighty prophet himself, he was content to be known as 'the friend of the bridegroom'. For John there was no greater honour than this – to be a friend of Jesus.

A friend of mine mentioned the name of another preacher to me and asked if I knew him. When I confessed that I didn't, he said to me, "He is known as the friend of the Holy Spirit". I was so moved! What a thing to be known as! What a reputation to have! Do I want to be known as a greater preacher, a great miracle worker, the leader of a great ministry? Or do I want to be known as the friend of the Holy Spirit? Do I want to be known as the friend of the bridegroom, the friend of God?

John tells us what it means to be a friend of the bridegroom:

> "The friend who attends the bridegroom waits and listens for Him" (v29).

This is what it is all about. Friendship with God means waiting on Him. Sitting at His feet. Building a tent of meeting. Walking with Him in the cool of the day. Going up the mountain. Spending that time free from all distractions and just waiting. And what are you waiting for? His voice. To hear Him speak. To hear the sound of Heaven.

And what is the fruit of this intimacy?

*"(he is) full of joy when he hears the bridegrooms voice. That joy is mine, and it is now complete" (v29).*

Joy is always the fruit of intimacy. For John there was no greater joy than hearing the voice of Jesus. For the true friend of the bridegroom, this is where our joy is found, communing with Him – this is ecstasy, this is bliss.

*"How sweet are Your words to my taste, sweeter than honey to my mouth!" (Psalm 119:103)*

*"When Your words came, I ate them; they were my joy and my heart's delight, for I bear Your name, Lord God Almighty." (Jeremiah 15:16)*

Hearing His voice has to become addictive to us. It has to be our greatest joy and our greatest delight. Nothing should taste sweeter. Nothing else should satisfy like hearing Him speak. Intimacy with Him should be our greatest longing and our greatest desire.

*"Bread alone will not satisfy, but true life is found in every word, which constantly goes forth from God's mouth." (Matthew 4:4 - TPT)*

Friendship with God, hearing His voice, catching the sound of heaven – this is our food. This is the thing that gives life. This is the thing that sustains us. This is what energises us. This is what we are hungry for. This is what we crave. We want to know Him and hear Him speak to us!

## The sound from the temple

As Jesus hung on the cross breathing His last, mankind was totally unaware that the greatest moment in all of human history was taking place. Whilst some were just going about their daily lives, others were at the foot of the cross, watching the death of Jesus of Nazareth. And then there were others, the religious leaders, who were gathered in the temple in Jerusalem getting on with their rituals and duties.

As Jesus died several sounds were heard. For those gathered around the cross, they heard the sound of Jesus crying out in a loud voice as He breathed His last. For everyone else in Jerusalem they heard the sound of rocks being split as the earth shook. The crucifixion was certainly not a quiet event!

But for those in the temple there was a different sound. A sound that would shake them to the core. It was the sound of the curtain in the temple being torn in two from top to bottom! (Matthew 27:51)

The thick curtain of religion that separated mankind from the holy of holies – the place of God's presence and glory was being opened up. God was making a way for all to enter His presence, for all to come close. For all to be His friends.

The sound of fabric ripping may have been a different noise to the sound of footsteps in a garden, or the noise of a ram's horn blasting, but it was the same sound – the sound of heaven inviting humanity into intimacy. The call to enter in and be a friend of God.

It is the same as the sound of knocking on a door.

*"Behold, I'm standing at the door, knocking. If your heart is open to hear My voice and you open the door within, I will come in to you and feast with you, and you will feast with Me." (Revelation 3:20)*

The church at Laodicea was outwardly rich, prosperous and successful but they had no room for the presence of Jesus. They were no longer interested in truly knowing Him. Now Jesus was actually outside this church, trying to get in.

I wonder if any of them could hear the sound of Him knocking? The sound of knocking was an invitation – open up, let me in. I want to be with you again. I want to dine with you. I am calling you to a close, intimate relationship as my friends.

Can you hear the sound of God walking in the garden? Can you hear the sound of the ram's horn blowing? Can you hear the sound of the curtain being torn? Can you hear the sound of Jesus knocking on the door? It's all the same sound – the sound of heaven crying, "I want you to know me! I want to talk with you, be with you. You can enjoy me, be one with me, hear my voice, know my presence. I am calling you to be my friend".

*"I no longer call you servants, because a servant does not know his master's business. Instead, I have called you friends, for everything that I learned from My Father I have made known to you." (John 15:15)*

When Jesus says He calls us friends, He is not just stating a fact – He is offering an opportunity. Friendship is something He calls us into, He invites us into. It is up to us whether we respond to that call.

But the rewards are incredible. As we enter into that friendship, He reveals to us His heart, His mind, His plans, His purposes.

> *"No one can come to me unless the Father who sent Me draws them, and I will raise them up at the last day. It is written in the Prophets: "They will all be taught by God." Everyone who has heard the Father and learned from Him comes to Me."*
> *(John 6:44-45)*

The longing of God is that He would be your teacher. That we would know what it is to receive revelation directly from Him.

But in order to do that we must come to Him. How do we come to Him? We respond to the drawing, the wooing. Jesus said that the Father is drawing us, then He says that we must "hear" the Father. He draws us with a sound. The sound of walking, the sound of the ram's horn, the sound of the veil being torn, the sound of knocking at the door. The sound inviting you into that place of intimacy where He can teach you and show you His heart.

Can you hear that sound? Will you respond? Will you come to Him, wait for Him, be with Him? This is the great longing of God!

## The sound from the fire

As John the Baptist stood in the waters of the River Jordan he invited people to be baptised in those waters. The invitation was not to be sprinkled but to be fully immersed in those waters, to literally become soaked in the river.

John prophesied a day when another Baptist would come:

*"I baptise you with water for repentance. But after me comes one who is more powerful than I, whose sandals I am not worthy to carry. He will baptise you with the Holy Spirit and fire." (Matthew 3:11)*

John the Baptist is in heaven, but Jesus the Baptist is here with us now. Jesus the Baptist is stood next to you right now as you read this book. Jesus doesn't stand in the River Jordan, but Jesus stands in a river of liquid fire that flows from the throne of God. Jesus wants to take you by the hand and fully immerse you in the river of fire! He wants you to be saturated, consumed, soaked in the fire of the Holy Spirit.

The fire is the Holy Spirit and the Holy Spirit is a person and the person has a voice.

*"The Lord spoke to you out of the fire" (Deuteronomy 4:12)*

*"Has any other people heard the voice of God speaking out of fire, as you have, and lived?" (Deuteronomy 4:33)*

An invitation to be baptised in fire is an invitation to hear His voice, to truly know Him. It's only in the fire, in the presence of the Holy Spirit that I can hear Him and know Him.

He is calling you into that fire right now. He is calling you to allow His fire to burn away everything that is not of Him, to enter the fiery presence of the Holy Spirit. Right now where you are, turn your thoughts to Jesus, turn your attention to Jesus, begin to worship Jesus. Tell the Lord that you love Him. "While I meditated the fire burned" (Psalm 39:3). Let that fire fall upon you now. Let that fire consume you. Enter the fire. Yield to it. And now in that place, let Him speak to you from within the fire. Lean in and listen to the sound of His voice.

## Deep calls to deep

*"As the deer pants for streams of water, so my soul pants for you, my God. My soul thirsts for God, for the living God. When can I go and meet with God? My tears have been my food day and night, while people say to me all day long, 'Where is your God?' These things I remember as I pour out my soul: how I used to go to the house of God under the protection of the Mighty One with shouts of joy and praise among the festive throng." (Psalm 42)*

Psalm 42 is the song of a man who has lost that sense of intimacy with God. He used to be a leader in the house of God, he used to enjoy the joy of praise and worship. But now all he has is a "used to". Maybe some of us can relate to that. We used to enjoy God's presence. We used to find joy in Bible reading. We used to have a passion for prayer. We used to hear His voice with clarity.

But now where is God? Have we lost Him? Can we find Him again?

"Deep calls to deep" (v7)

But still, there is a sound. It may have faded, it may seem distant but that sound never stops calling, never stops pursuing us. It is two sounds. It is sound from the depths of God calling us into friendship and intimacy. And from the depths of the Psalmist comes a cry, a longing to meet with God. These two sounds call out to one another like an echo – God longing for humanity, humanity longing for God, deep calling unto deep.

As the Psalmist responds to that pull, that wooing to enter the depths of God's love, the depths of God's glory, He describes what He can hear as being like the sound of the roar of a waterfall. It's an awesome, majestic sound. A roaring, a thundering. Almost terrifying. Ear splitting. The sound of water pounding down on the rocks. It's a furious sound. A mighty sound.

Under the wave of His waterfalls, He washes away our fears, our sins, our apathy, our religion, our dullness. It's an awesome, almost frightening moment.

But as we yield to this process, the furious sound of the waterfall begins to cease and we hear another sound.

> *"By day the Lord directs His love, at night His song is with me" (v8)*

The roar of His waterfalls makes way for His tender love song. Like a conductor, God himself directs Heaven to sing a song of love over me. A song of romance, a song of intimacy. The song above all songs. The song that sings, "You are mine and I love you".

Many of us never hear that sound because we run away at the sound of the waterfalls. But yield to Heaven's process. Let Him batter and chip away all that is not of Him. Let Him wash away the dullness so that you can hear His sweet song of love over you.

This is what it is all about – the steps in the garden, the horn on the mountain, the veil being ripped, the knock at the door, the thunder of the waterfall – all of heaven making as much noise as possible to get our attention. "I want you! I want to be your friend! I want to sing a love song over you!"

Can you hear it? Are you listening? Heaven is calling. It's time to respond.

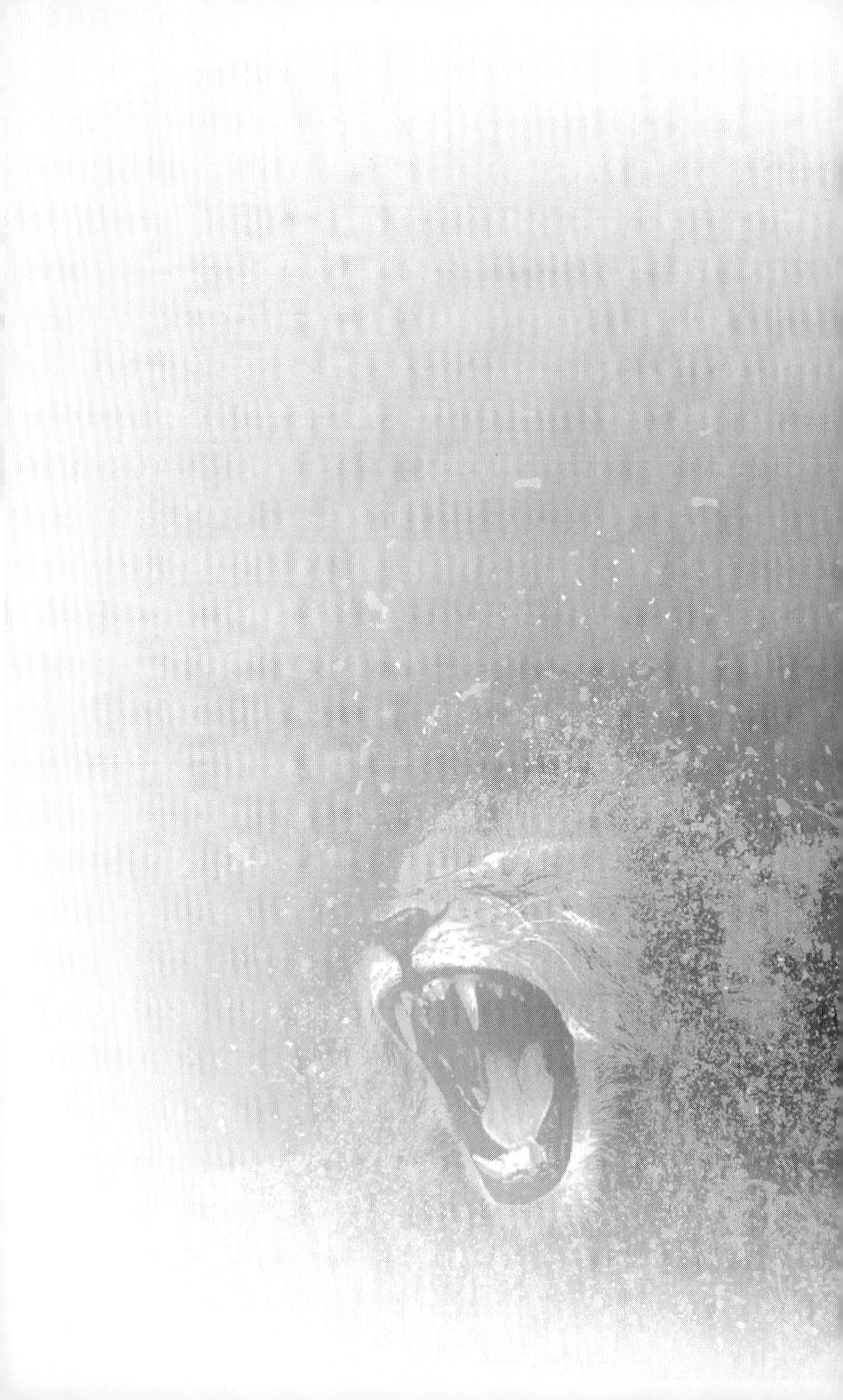

# THE SOUND OF REVIVAL

*"As I was prophesying, there was a noise, a rattling sound, and the bones came together, bone to bone" (Ezekiel 37:7)*

When Christians talk about "the presence of God" it may be helpful to explain what exactly we mean by that. Even Christians themselves can sometimes be confused as to what exactly the presence of God is.

Theologically I believe that when we speak about God's presence there are three different things that we can be referring to.

The first is God's omnipresence. This is the theological truth that God's presence is everywhere, all the time. Unlike man, God is not limited by geography, time or space but He manages to be everywhere all at once, at the same time.

However, there is another level, a deeper experience of God's presence and that is His indwelling presence. This is where God's presence has come and set up home within Christians. This is very different to His omnipresence as it is something that only God's children can experience. But for those us of us who are born again, God's Spirit lives within us and we have the promise that He will never leave.

Although God is omnipresent, the reality is that most people on the planet are unaware of His presence. It is even true of Christians that although He is always in us, we sometimes have to live this out by faith as we can't always feel God or see Him at work.

This brings us to another aspect of God's presence – God's manifest presence. This is when the presence of God is felt or experienced. When God's presence is manifest for an extended period of time, we often call it "revival". Revival can come to an individual – this is when a backslidden or lukewarm believer returns to their first love. They suddenly feel like they have born again "again" – their passion for God, their hunger for Him, a sense of closeness to God, feelings of joy, an ease in prayer – all of these things have been "revived" in their lives.

Revival can also come to a local church too. Signs of revival in a church will include individuals being revived, as mentioned above, but also other signs as well. Quite often these include a greater awareness of God's presence in corporate gatherings often with signs, wonders and miracles taking place. Souls will be saved, the Church will grow, prodigals will return. Lives will be changed as God pours out His Spirit. People will make a conscious effort to live holy as conviction of sin becomes very real.

Revival can sometimes come too, not only to a local church but to a larger geographical area. This could be to a town, a region or even a nation. It is when this happens that the entire spiritual climate or atmosphere of an area can change. Now churches throughout that area begin to be touched by God and they begin to work together as a move of unity takes place. A wider revival like this won't just affect churches but will affect society itself as moral and social changes that are in line with God's Word will begin to come into effect.
There have been many stories over the past two thousand years of all of these different expressions of revival. Other terms we could use would be reformation,

outpouring, an awakening or a visitation. I personally prefer to speak in terms of the Kingdom of God coming to earth. However, I accept that through Church history the word "revival" is the term most commonly used to these special manifestations of God's presence and glory.

## Sounds in a graveyard

In Ezekiel 37 there is a powerful passage that speaks of the future revival of the nation of Israel. God uses a very graphic picture to show His people what will take place.

God takes the prophet Ezekiel and places him in the middle of a valley full of dry bones. The bones are dry and disconnected. Everywhere Ezekiel looks all he can see is death. There are no visible signs of life whatsoever.

In the midst of that God asks the prophet this question, "Son of man, can these bones live?" He is asking Ezekiel, "Can revival come to this seemingly hopeless situation?"

For those who are familiar with the text we know the answer and we know the end of the story! Yes, revival can come to a graveyard! The story ends with the bones coming together and flesh appearing, then breath comes and finally they stand together as a vast army!

God is showing His people that what He did to these dry bones is exactly what He will do for them. Although in the present Israel was saying, "Our bones are dried up and our hope is gone; we are cut off." (v11), there would come a day when God would "open your graves and bring you up from them. I will put My Spirit in you and you will live" (v13-14).

Ezekiel would play a major role in the revival of the dry bones as God would command him to prophesy the revival into being, but notice what happened as Ezekiel prophesied:

> "As I was prophesying, there was a noise, a rattling sound, and the bones came together, bone to bone." (v8)

At this point in the narrative the revival hadn't yet fully come – but before it did, there was a sound!

In the midst of a valley surrounded by death, this prophet of God began to hear a sound. It was the sound of bones coming together, a rattling sound. It was the sound of that which had been disconnected coming together again. It was the sound of unity, the sound of realignment, the sound of things coming back into their proper place and order. It was the sound of hope!

As Ezekiel continued to prophecy there was another sound, the sound of wind, of breath, in Hebrew "ruach" – the sound of the Holy Spirit. This was the sound of resurrection life and power.

These sounds preceded the army rising up and the nation being restored. The sound was the indicator that revival was coming. The sound was the sign that a move of God was about to take place!

## The sound of rain

As we look throughout Church history we see that revival is often preceded by a "sound". After all it is true that "Surely the Sovereign Lord does nothing without revealing His plan to His servants the prophets." (Amos 3:7)

Prior to every move of God there have been prophetic people who somehow have managed to hear the sound of heaven and they have a sense that God is about to do something incredible. These men and women who have heard the sound of heaven are often responsible for sharing this sound with others and for helping to pray it and prophesy it into being.

In 1 Kings 18 the nation of Israel has been in a three and half year drought. For all this time there has not been a drop of rain on the land. Then there comes a powerful moment when the prophet Elijah confronts King Ahab.

> "Then Elijah said to Ahab, "Go up, eat and drink; for there is the sound of abundance of rain" (v41)

It is important to be aware that at this point there still hadn't been a drop of rain or even a cloud in the sky!

I wonder if Ahab looked up at the clear blue sky and felt the hot Middle Eastern sun on his skin and wondered if this prophet had gone mad!

Yet Elijah could hear something that Ahab couldn't see. In the Kingdom what you hear is always more important than what you can see for "we live by faith, not by sight" (2 Corinthians 5:7) and "faith comes from hearing" (Romans 10:17). What you hear is always more important than what is visible. Elijah was in tune with heaven. He could hear it in the spirit realm – the sound of an abundance of rain. He knew God was about to move!

In response to this sound from heaven, Elijah went up the mountain to seek God. With his head between his knees (the Middle Eastern birthing position) Elijah begins to pray and intercede so that what he can hear in the spirit realm will be manifest on earth. Seven times Elijah cries out to God until finally his servant brings him news that a cloud "the size of a man's hand" has appeared. Elijah knows that God has heard and that breakthrough has come.

The passage ends with the sky becoming black and a mighty downpour of rain just like Elijah said would happen.

Today there are some who look at the Church globally or who look at the nations of the world and all the injustice and unrighteousness and like Ahab they can see no signs of revival. To them all seems hopeless. But then there are others who can hear a sound from heaven, a sign that God is about to pour out His Spirit in a way that mankind has never seen before.

## Revival prophesy

In January 2007 I had felt led to go away and spend some time seeking God for an encounter with His presence. For several days I prayed and fasted, waiting on God for a personal revival that I knew I needed. On the last night, the manifest presence of God came into that room. For a few hours I lay prostrate on the floor as fire flowed through my body and I shook as the Holy Spirit filled me over and over again.

It was in that moment that I began to catch something of the sound of heaven about what God wanted to do in this generation. I began to hear the sound of a future revival that would touch children and teenagers. As I began to hear this sound, I began to write and these are the words that flowed.

*My power and glory is going to invade youth and children's ministries, so much so that they will no longer be known as just "youth meetings" or "children's church", but revival hubs, places of encounter.*

*Young people will come not for games, activities or social events but purely for the fire of God's Spirit.*

*People will walk into youth meetings and children's services who have never been to church before and ask "what must I do to be saved?"*

*Young people will beg for the meetings not to finish. Others will leave and come back, bringing their friends, mothers and fathers and grandparents.*

*The fire of God will be so tangible in these services. There will be youth meetings that will transition into all night prayer meetings.*

*There will be no break between youth meetings and the main church services, the youth meetings will simply run into the Sunday morning church gathering. As soon as church members enter the building, even those who have only ever known religion will be touched by the fire of God.*

*Parents, school teachers and local reporters will flock to these gatherings. Some out of curiosity, some out of concern and some out of anger. But just as when King Saul and his men came to kill David, the power of God shall fall on them and they shall be overwhelmed by the Spirit.*

*The lame will be brought in wheelchairs by the unsaved and they will say "we have heard that the God of miracles is in this place!" There will be an outbreak of signs and wonders and the healing power of God.*

*In those days the power of God will be so strong that men and women will get up to speak the word of God and as soon as they open their mouths large groups of people will be overwhelmed and fall under the power of the Spirit of God.*
*Parents will bring their children who are addicted to drugs and they will leave set free. Children will bring their alcoholic parents and they will be set free. People will travel great distances to see these things.*

*Young people will go directly from the meetings to their school and as they enter their classroom the glory of God will be so strong that teachers will break down weeping under the conviction of the Holy Spirit. Men who have taught evolution and atheism in public, will in public beg for forgiveness as they admit that they were wrong.*

*This will be a faceless revival, carried by young people – children and teenagers with pure hearts and a simple faith, unadulterated by the religion of the previous generations. Young people full of the fire of the Holy Spirit.*

*For a season, the baptismal tank will remain open on a daily basis as whole families go through the waters at the same time.*

*The carriers of this revival will be so full of the fire that they will enter shops and* supermarkets and people will weep under the conviction of the Holy Spirit. Miracles, signs and wonders will take place in public – in shops, on the streets and as children play with their friends in parks and at sports games.

The behaviour of some so called "troubled" young people will change so drastically that head teachers of schools and government officials will come seeking answers as did the Queen of Sheba. This will open up doors of influence for my Church on a governmental level as youth and children's pastors are called in to help solve social problems on a national scale.

This will be a time when God's grace and mercy are shown to many. However, this will also be a time of great persecution. Many from outside the Church and inside the church will display their wrath and anger at what God is doing. However, press on. Do not give in. His judgement will be sure and His retribution swift. "I cannot be mocked says the Lord God of Hosts".

In those days the servants of God will possess such an authority that the mouths of the critics, cynics and opponents will be silenced and there will be no doubt that something divine and supernatural is taking place.

The wrath of many will be so fierce that you will feel shaken to the core. However, know that you are in the centre of His hands. He will hold, shield and protect His servants.

The worship in those days will be so powerful that the angels of God will encamp around the building in wonder. Children and young people will not look to a band or a worship leader to lead them. The praise and worship will be spontaneous, flowing out of hearts of love and devotion to God.

*In those days, musicians and singers will open their mouths but be overcome with glory and be unable to minister. However the worship will continue regardless. A preacher will get up to speak but be unable to open his mouth and yet people will still come to salvation. Then you will truly know that He is the Lord of Heaven, the Sovereign Lord, and He is a limitless, all powerful God.*

*Broadcasts of these services will be played in homes, schools and even pubs and as soon as young people, children and teenagers, come on screen, testifying to the works of God, people will turn to the Saviour.*

*This will not just be about one youth group or ministry, neither will there be one preacher known as the leader of the revival. Instead, men and women of like-minded spirit will gather together and there will be services of this kind, held for young people up and down the land. These will initially be held in churches and as they are outgrown will transition into theatres and public halls. Eventually the largest stadiums and auditoriums in the land will hold these mass gatherings of children and teenagers who are hungry for God.*

*Out of this generation of young people God will raise up mighty intercessors. There prayers will have so much authority and be so in-line with His Spirit that the prayers of this generation will influence cities, governments and even nations.*

It was this word and sound from heaven that would shape my life and ministry. In retrospect I believe that God is saying the following.

*The Spirit of God is urging senior pastors and leaders to think carefully who they place in charge of their children's and youth's programmes. Do not just appoint people who can run a meeting for young people, but look to strategically place revivalists over your youth and children's programmes who can prepare this generation for the move of God's Spirit and help steward and father what God is going to do. These personnel and staffing decisions are absolutely essential. I believe the Lord is saying it is a time for a strategic assembling and positioning of my generals who are being brought into position for such a time as this.*

*I believe the Lord is urging youth pastors and children's pastors – prepare this generation for what I am going to do. You are not running a programme for young people – you are spearheading a revival. The preaching of My Word and what you preach is the essential part of this preparation. You must preach hunger, you must preach purity, you must impart the fire of God.*

## Jarrod Cooper

I am by no means the only person to have heard a sound from heaven that God is about to do something extraordinary on the earth. The senior leader of our home church, Jarrod Cooper also had a powerful encounter with the glory of God where he heard this "sound" of revival. He writes:

*In 1996 I encountered the glory of God in a six-week visit to South Africa. In that time I was filled with a vision for the United Kingdom and Europe. Night after night I awoke, day after day I prayed, and visions of a great revival were burned into my heart. I am convinced the Church must be ready to host a glory at a level previously unknown.*

*The presence of God is preparing to sweep across Europe as never seen before. It will be in response to the apostolic reformation currently underway. Stadiums, arenas and the greatest auditoriums will be turned into church buildings. Market places filled with thousands will be overcome by the glory of God. The blind will see. The lame will walk. Street evangelism will happen as never seen before, as mass healings take place on street corners and in shopping centres. Where many have spent years sowing, others will reap on a massive scale.*

*God's glory will touch the media, politics and royalty. His glory will invade live TV shows, as men and women of God reveal the power of God in healings, strange signs and prophetic words and wisdom. Many politicians will come to Christ in a very visible way. For some this will bring prominence, for others ridicule and scandal. Governments and kings will call days of prayer.*

*Thousands will stream into the Kingdom of God as a great move of signs and wonders floods our churches, work places and homes. Some believers will be transfigured as Moses was. Trances, dreams and visions will become common place. The weather will be controlled by believers at certain times, and used as a sign to communities where they are ministering. Neighbours will knock on the doors of those known to be Christians, begging to be led to Christ and to find peace for their souls. Many businesses and work places will hold prayer meetings; some will even close for whole days of prayer. Study groups will meet at all hours of the day in business establishments.*

*The glory of God will fill the greatest auditoriums in the land as Christians try to find places to gather that can contain the numbers flooding into the Kingdom. Great and glorious signs and wonders will be performed by apostolic teams, though even the least among the Church will see miracles as common place. Churches will be planted on a daily basis. Leaders will be trained quickly and released easily. Youngsters will lead churches of hundreds and thousands. A softening of hearts between generations in churches will mean all ages will worship and walk together.*

*In the coming move of God's glory in the earth, worship ministry will change greatly, not so much because of our own skill and design, but because men and women will be so overwhelmed by the presence of God. At times, whole bands will physically collapse under the weight of his presence. On occasions, crowds will stream out of auditoriums, terrified as God's glory is revealed in clouds, "writings on the wall" (Daniel 5), earthquakes, audible voices and manifestations of angelic beings.*

*In local churches many congregations will worship and sing without formal worship/ music ministries. There will simply be too many Christians to be served by musical bands. People will meet from house to house, where spontaneous worship will flow on led by the Spirit himself. Singing in tongues and intercessions will last for hours and days at a time. Leaders will often take a back seat and let God lead his people, trusting the intensity of His holiness and presence to keep the meetings in some sense of heavenly "order". The revival will be known as a "leaderless" one in many places, as the glory of God will rest on the corporate Church, rather than just a few prominent figures.*

*Every expression of worship, from extravagant foolishness, to tender quietness, will flow like waves through churches. Denominational barriers, styles and wrong authority structures will break down in many communities and countries, leaving the Church full of variety and flavour, but without barriers and comparison.*

*Wonderful worship bands, anointed to facilitate God's presence and move in the prophetic will be raised up. Albums that seem to capture the very intensity of God's presence will be used to impact millions. Radio and TV will open up to Christian music and feature glorious worship times with signs and wonders. These broadcasts will impact many households, and through the medium of T.V. millions will be saved, experiencing the presence of God in worship.*

*Some communities will feature 24-hour worship times, lasting for months and even years. Some of these will become incredible "hot spots" of God's glory, and the light of God's presence will be physically seen from miles around at times. Many people, saved and unsaved, will be overwhelmed by God's Spirit when attempting to travel near these places. There will be 100% success rates in praying for the sick in some of these communities, a fact that will result in thousands visiting for prayer. Kings and presidents will visit them and find their hearts melting, touched by the glory of God during worship.*

## Smith Wigglesworth

In 1947, the great healing evangelist Smith Wigglesworth was praying with his friend Lester Sumrall when he began to hear a sound of a revival that would take place in the future.

*There will be the biggest move of the Holy Spirit that the nation (Great Britain), and indeed, the world has ever seen. It will mark the beginning of a revival that will eclipse anything that has been witnessed within these shores, even the Wesleyan and Welsh revivals of former years. The outpouring of God's Spirit will flow over from the United Kingdom to mainland Europe, and from there, will begin a missionary move to the ends of the earth.*

*I see the greatest revival in the history of mankind coming to planet earth, maybe as never before. And I see every form of disease healed. I see whole hospitals emptied with no one there. Even the doctors are running down the streets shouting. They will bring the sick to churches where they allow the Holy Ghost to move.*

*There will be untold numbers of uncountable multitudes that would be saved. No man will say 'so many, so many,' because nobody will be able to count those who come to Jesus. No disease will be able to stand before God's people. It will be a worldwide situation, not local. A worldwide thrust of God's power and God's anointing upon mankind.*

## John G Lake

In 1931, the great apostle John G Lake saw a vision from heaven. He wrote:

*I saw a company of men walk out, and I saw all the diseases and all the crimes and agonies. I saw cancers and tumours and tuberculous, and I saw a company of men and women walk down in the midst of it, and I heard them say, "Here comes the sons of God. Here comes the conquerors."*

*And the sons of God said to disease, "In the name of Jesus, depart" and disease fled. It fled as it did before the Son of God. It obeyed because the son of God sent them out and gave them His name as authority. I saw the company of men enter into the lost dominion and walked out as conquerors over death and hell and the grave. They were masters. They were rulers.*

## The sound of revival

These prophetic words are just a handful of literally thousands of words from heaven that many believe are referring to our time, to our generation.

As you read through these prophecies can you hear the sound from heaven? Is your spirit being stirred to believe that God is "about to do something…that will make the ears of everyone who hears about it tingle"? (1 Samuel 3:11)

We have not yet seen the fulfilment of everything that God wants to do in this generation, although I believe we are seeing a cloud as small as a man's hand. But in my spirit I know that more is coming! I can hear the sound of an abundance of rain!

Will you join me up the mountain? Will you join in me seeking God, crying out for His Kingdom to come and joining in with the prayer of old:

*"Will you not revive us again, that Your people may rejoice in You?" (Psalm 85:6)*

In 2010, my brother Matthew was working for an evangelistic ministry that was preaching the gospel around the world. They were scheduled to minister at a conference that was being held in a church in Alabama in the USA. This meeting turned into what became known as "The Bay of the Holy Spirit" revival as thousands of salvations and notable healings took place over several months.

A few months into this revival I flew over for a few days to see what God was doing. The meetings were large – but I had been in big meetings before. The worship was great – but I had been in powerful times of worship before. The preaching was powerful – but I had heard powerful preaching before. Salvations and miracles were certainly taking place, but again I had seen salvations and healings in other places too. What was different that I not experienced before? The sound! On this trip I learnt that revival has a distinct sound. If you've never experienced it, it is like trying to describe the sound of thunder to a person who was born deaf. Almost impossible. Some things you just have to experience for yourself!

Revival certainly has a unique sound, just something in the atmosphere that sounds different.

In the years since then I have been privileged in my own ministry to have little tastes of moves of God in Africa, Europe, Central and Southern America. I have been in powerful meetings but revival is different, it has a different sound and a different feel.

I have been in altar calls in Africa where the sounds of repentance have filled the air as hundreds of precious souls have in tears given their lives to Jesus. In Argentina the sounds of laughter and dancing were heard as God swept through a town that was known in the local language as "the house of pain". In Mexico I have heard the sound of spontaneous worship as crowds of people were overwhelmed by the presence of God and had to respond with singing. The sounds of salvation. The sounds of healing testimonies. The sounds of prayer and intercession. The sounds of glory. This is what I live for!

There is just a unique and distinct sound when heaven invades earth and His presence is made manifest.

In Jeremiah 25 God speaks of how the nation of Israel would go into 70 years of Babylonian captivity because of their disobedience. One of the signs of their bondage would be:

*"I will banish from them the sounds of joy and gladness, the voices of bride and bridegroom, the sound of millstones and the light of the lamp. This whole country*

*will become a desolate wasteland, and these nations will serve the king of Babylon for seventy years." (Jeremiah 25:10-11)*

As God's people backslide and were under judgement there would be an eerie sound of silence, an eerie sound of the inactivity of heaven.

A dead church is surely one in which there is no sound. Now, don't confuse a lack of noise with a lack of sound! Noise is surface level. The sound that this book is about is spiritual, it is more powerful than noise.

I have been is noisy churches that have had the sound of death in them. Likewise I have been in meetings where for hours people have been in complete silence and yet the atmosphere is pregnant with the sound from heaven. One man of God calls it "living stillness". In the silence, a sound is being heard.

After 70 years in Babylonian captivity God would restore the nation of Israel. Jeremiah prophesies about this restoration in chapter 33. And guess what would accompany this revival? A sound!

> *"The sounds of joy and gladness, the voices of bride and bridegroom, and the voices of those who bring thank offerings to the house of the Lord, saying, 'Give thanks to the Lord Almighty, for the Lord is good; his love endures for ever.' For I will restore the fortunes of the land as they were before," says the Lord. 'This is what the Lord Almighty says: "In this place, desolate and without people or animals – in all its towns there will again be pastures for shepherds to rest their flocks. (v11-12)*

As revival came to the nation, the nation was again filled with the sounds of heaven! The sounds of laughter, the sounds of love and intimacy, the sounds of worship and praise filled the air!

Do you believe that a nation or city can be filled with a different sound? The sounds of injustice, of perversion, of division, of hatred, of corruption being drowned out by the sound of heaven! This is what happened in Acts 8 as Philip preached the gospel in a particular place and great joy filled the city (v8). Things sounded differently than they did the day before!

Revival is preceded by a sound and revival is accompanied by a sound. Can you hear it? Do you long to hear it?

I close this chapter with the lyrics of this powerful prophetic song written by singer / songwriter Martin Smith:

> Did you feel the mountains tremble?
> Did you hear the oceans roar?
> When the people rose to sing of
> Jesus Christ, the risen One
>
> Did you feel the people tremble?
> Did you hear the singers roar?
> When the lost began to sing of
> Jesus Christ, the saving One
>
> And we can see that God You're moving
> A mighty river through the nations

And young and old will turn to Jesus

Fling wide you heavenly gates
Prepare the way of the risen Lord

Open up the doors and let the music play
Let the streets resound with singin'
Songs that bring Your hope and
Songs that bring Your joy
Dancers who dance upon injustice

Do you feel the darkness tremble
When all the saints join in one song?
And all the streams flow as one river
To wash away our brokenness

Written by Martin Smith ©1995 Curious? Music UK

# THE SOUND OF THE IMPOSTER

*"The gatekeeper opens the gate for him, and the sheep listen to his voice. He calls his own sheep by name and leads them out. When he has brought out all his own, he goes on ahead of them, and his sheep follow him because they know his voice."*
*(John 10:3-4)*

As we have already discussed, Jesus our Good Shepherd directs us by the sound of His voice. In the Middle East, shepherds would not come behind the sheep and drive them, but instead would walk ahead of them and call them. As the sheep listened to and responded to the voice of their shepherd, he would direct them to safety and to pasture. Failure to correctly listen to the voice of the shepherd could lead to disaster.

Again, it is important to understand that sheep don't understand words as such; it is the sound of the shepherds voice that becomes familiar to them. In his book "A Shepard looks at the Good Shepherd", Phillip Keller writes:

*"The relationship which rapidly develops between a shepherd and the sheep under his care is to a definite degree dependent upon the use of the shepherd's voice. Sheep quickly become accustomed to their owner's particular voice. They are*

*acquainted with its unique tone. They know its particular sounds and inflections. They can distinguish it from that of any other person".*

This is a very important lesson for us to understand. Many times, we think because something seems to be accurate and correct that it is God speaking. This is not necessarily the case. A sermon may be doctrinally sound, a prophetic word may contain elements of truth, advice may seem to be solid – but whose sound is behind it? Is it the sound, the voice, of the Good Shepherd? We have to be so intimate with the Shepherd that we don't just know facts about Him and His Word, but we know the voice behind the truth, the sound contained within the Scripture.

Keller goes on to say:

*"If a stranger should come among them, they would not recognise nor respond to his voice in the same way they would to that of the shepherd. Even if the visitor should use the same words and phrases as that of their rightful owner they would not react in the same way. It is a case of becoming actually conditioned to the familiar nuances and personal accent of their shepherd's call"*

As you can imagine, this kind of relationship requires a closeness to the shepherd that can only come from spending time with him.

Jesus confirms, "they will never follow a stranger; in fact, they will run away from him because they do not recognise a stranger's voice." (v5)

There are two voices that compete for the sheep's attention and obedience – the voice of the shepherd and the voice of the stranger.

A wise sheep correctly discerns the sound of the shepherd's voice and will respond by following that sound. The result is safety and good pasture. A sheep that is fooled into thinking that the voice of the stranger is that of the shepherd however is in great danger. Whereas the sound of the shepherd's voice leads to life, following the sound of the strangers voice always results in death and destruction (v10).

Keller continues:

*"It used to amaze and intrigue visitors to my ranches to discover that my sheep were so indifferent to their voices. Occasionally I would invite them to call my sheep using the same words and phrases which I habitually employed. But it was to no avail. The ewes and lambs, would simply stand and stare at the newcomers in rather blank bewilderment, as if to say, "who are you?"*

*This is simply because over a period of time sheep come to associate the sound of the shepherd's voice with special benefits. When the shepherd calls to them it is for a specific purpose that has their own best interests in mind. It is not something he does just to indulge himself or pass the time away.*

*His voice is used to announce his presence; he is there. It is to allay their fears and timidity. Or it is to call them to himself so they can be examined and counted carefully. He wants to make sure they are all well, fit and flourishing. Sometimes the voice is used to announce that fresh feed is being supplied, or salt, minerals or water. He might call them up to lead them into fresh pastures or into some shelter from an approaching storm. But always the master's call conveys to the sheep a positive assurance that he cares for them and is acting in their best interests."*

How vital it is that we learn to discern the voice of the shepherd from that of any imposter and that we respond correctly to that voice.

Make no mistake about it, for every one of us there are different voices that compete for our attention and our allegiance.

It is interesting that although Jesus talks of the stranger and the thief in the singular, He says "all who ever came before me were thieves and robbers but the sheep did not listen to them" (v8) – indicating many voices. Jesus seems to be indicating that although there is one source to these foreign sounds, satan himself, he communicates using many voices. These can be the voices of our past, the voice of shame, doubt, unbelief, fear, unworthiness, jealousy, condemnation etc. We could go on.

## Who do you respond to?

A few weeks ago, I took my two children to a local park for the afternoon. It is a park we've been to many times before and on this particular day we along with many others were enjoying the uncharacteristic British sunshine as we played on the swings and slides. What I didn't know was that this park had a speaker system which meant that someone in an office somewhere could broadcast messages throughout the park.

Around 4.00 pm the speaker system kicked in and a man's voice declared, "This park will be closing its gates in one hour. If you could kindly leave the park before then or else you will be locked in overnight. Thank you for your corporation."

Interestingly as I looked around none of the children in the park paid this voice any attention whatsoever. They ignored this mild threat and carried on playing regardless, not allowing this request to interfere with their fun. For the adults like myself it was a different matter. After the man had finished speaking, I began to pack up our things and gathered my children as we prepared to leave.

As we were exiting the park, the strangest thing happened. The speaker came on again but this time it was the voice of a little girl laughing. I immediately guessed that somehow an imposter had broken into the office of wherever the microphone was. The little girl and her accomplice who seemed a similar age then shouted over the microphone, "You are all going to die! I'm going to kill you", before more laughter and the broadcast suddenly ending.

It was a bizarre episode. What was interesting though was the reaction in the park. This time all the adults ignored the girl's threat. Like me, they knew that this was a harmless prank. Maybe not very funny, but these girls had no power and no authority; it was an empty threat. Some parents even saw the funny side and began to laugh.

The children in the park though thought differently. Many of them began to scream and run away, convinced that they were about to be killed by some lunatic!

Afterwards, as I thought about this incident, I thought how the immature failed to recognise which was the voice of truth and which was the voice of an imposter. The mature among us though recognised only one voice has power and authority in this situation – the voice of the first man – that is the voice I will respond to. The second voice was the voice of an imposter. Its threat was empty, its power an illusion. I cannot therefore give this voice the time of day. I cannot allow it to produce fear within me. I cannot and will not be moved by the voice of the imposter.

Everyday many of us have the speaker system of our spirits hijacked by an imposter. The imposter comes in speaking words of doubt, fear, lies and unbelief. The imposter tries to speak words that contradict what God says about Himself, about us and about our circumstance.

The problem is that many of us mistake the voice of the imposter as the voice of truth. We allow his words to create fear within us and we respond to and are moved by his voice. Instead we have to understand that only God's voice is the voice of truth. Only His voice can I allow to be planted in my spirit. Only His voice should move and direct me.

All other voices must be identified for what they are – an imposter. And as such they have to be ignored.

In John 14:17, Jesus described the Holy Spirit as "The Spirit of truth". Only the Holy Spirit is the voice of truth in our lives. Everything He says is 100%, undiluted truth. Any voice that doesn't find its source from the Holy Spirit is a lie or at best a mixture of truth and lie.

We live in a world that is constantly searching for truth. Liberals tell us that our feelings are truth. The Word of God of course disputes this, telling us that our hearts are deceptive and wicked. As a contrast, conservatives tell us that it is not our feelings but facts that are truth. However, this is also a faulty interpretation. Although facts are one level of truth, there is a higher level of truth than even facts – and that is the Word of God and the voice of the Holy Spirit.

His Word is total truth and it is greater than our hearts and even the facts that we are faced with. Facts may say that we are sick, but truth says that "by His stripes we are healed". Facts may say I have an addiction, but truth says, "He who the Son sets free is free indeed". Facts may say I am broke, but truth says, "He is my provider".

Abraham, "faced the fact that his body was as good as dead....Yet he did not waver through unbelief regarding the promise of God, but was strengthened in his faith and gave glory to God" (Romans 4:19-20)

When the facts scream at us over the speaker system of our lives, it is so easy to believe that that is truth and respond with doubts and fear. But we must learn: any external voice that is not the voice of God is an imposter and I must ignore it. I cannot allow it to take root in my heart.

Of the Spirit of truth, Jesus said, "You know Him, for He lives with you and will be in you". Whereas the imposter's voice comes from outside of us, the voice of truth comes from deep within us, bearing witness to what God's Word has said over our lives. Jesus goes on to say "I will not leave you as orphans" (v18).

Jesus's solution to fatherlessness is to send us the Spirit of truth. How can we know that it is the voice of truth speaking to us? Because the Holy Spirit will only ever confirm our adoption as children of God. The Holy Spirit speaks to us of our identity as God's children. The Holy Spirit reaffirms who He are, who God is to us and what is available to us as part of our inheritance in Christ.

This is linked with what Jesus said in John 10: "He calls his own sheep by name" (v3). The Good Shepherd calls us by our names, by our true identity. In contrast, the sound of the imposter results in us questioning our identity and who we belong to.

Any voice that results in questions like "Am I really a child of God?", "Am I really forgiven?", "Is God really with me?", "Is healing really for me?", "Can I really approach God like a Father" – we can be sure that the source of this sound is an imposter and his voice has to be rejected.

But the voice that calls me by name, the voice that reaffirms who I am and whose I am – this is the voice of truth, and the only voice that I can trust and the only voice that I respond to.

*"The Holy Spirit....will remind you of everything I have said to you. Peace I leave with you; My peace I give you" (v26-27)*

Again, the Holy Spirit, His voice only comes to confirm everything Jesus has said about us. He comes to remind us of every promise that Jesus has made and everything that is available in Him. The sound of heaven always results in peace and wholeness. The voice of the imposter only brings fear and confusion.

## Identity Theft

In the UK in order to watch television you need to buy a license from the government. This has to be renewed each year. Last Christmas I was watching TV when an email pinged through saying that my television license had run out and I had to renew or else face prosecution. Getting my wallet out I began to fill in my bank details so that payment could go out. Just before I submitted the form, I had a nagging feeling in my stomach that something wasn't quite right. I asked my wife and sure enough she confirmed that the money for this year's television license had already gone out of our account. It was a scam! I was glad I had checked. A few weeks later, on the news came a report of a couple who had fallen victim to this scam and it had cost them their life savings!

They say that one of the fastest growing kinds of crime is identity theft. Thieves know that if they can steal your identity then they can get access to your bank details and other personal information, potentially scamming you out of everything.

In fact, identity theft is not a new phenomenon. Satan is the original identity thief. When he appeared to Adam and Eve in the garden what did he say? "Eat from this tree and you shall be like God" (Genesis 3). Of course, we know that Adam and Eve were already like God for they were created in His image and likeness. But there was satan, trying to get Adam and Eve to doubt and question their identity. He knew that if he could bring doubts into who God said they were, he could gain access into every area of their lives.

Jesus Himself almost became a victim of the identity thief. In Matthew 3, as Jesus began His ministry at the waters of baptism, heaven opens and a sound from heaven is heard. It is the sound of the voice of the Father, declaring over Jesus, "This is my Son, whom I love; with Him I am well pleased" (v17).

It was this declaration of His identity that became the launching pad for Jesus' ministry. But immediately following this, satan comes to tempt Him, and what is the first thing satan says? "If you are the Son of God, tell these stones to become bread" (Matthew 4:3).

What is satan doing? He is trying to steal Jesus' identity. He is trying to get Jesus to question who the Father has said He is. If he can just bring some doubt into Jesus' mind as to who God says that He is, he knows he has gained access into His life. But Jesus is not so easily fooled. His response "it is written" shows how Jesus responded to the voice of every imposter and identity thief – He always went back to the original source – God's Word. What has the Father said? What has the Father declared? What has the Father spoken? Jesus has the echo of His Father's voice, "You are my son", ringing in His ears and He refused to give any attention to or be side-tracked by any imposter.

*"He who sent Me is trustworthy, and what I have heard from Him I tell the world." (John 8:26)*

All Jesus' thoughts were Father-filtered. He could not afford to allow any voice into His life that wasn't the voice of the Father.

Every day our lives are filled with all kinds of sounds. Those sounds often take the form of voices that compete for our attention. We have to recognise the source of these sounds. Which sounds are from the imposter and which are from my Father? The imposter always brings fear, doubt and confusion. The Father always brings clarity, confirmation and affirmation. The imposter always addresses me as a stranger and an orphan. The Father always addresses me as a friend and as a son/daughter. The imposter steals from my life. The Father is the only One that brings peace, joy and security.

We have to allow any thought that isn't from the Father to pass us by. But the thoughts that come from the Father are the ones that we pick up from the conveyor belt of our minds and meditate on. Bill Johnson puts it so well: "I cannot afford thoughts in my head about me that God doesn't have in His".

Arriving at my church on Sunday morning I was told, "we have sound problems this morning". Apparently, things didn't 'sound' right. Now in such situations I am completely clueless but thankfully we have sound experts as part of the team. They can quickly identify which sounds are right and which are wrong. They cut off the wrong sounds, get rid of any negative interference and amplify the right sounds.

Whilst most us don't have the skill set to be on the sound desk at an event or public gathering, we all have to learn to sit behind the sound desk of our own lives. I have to know what it is to identify sounds that come from the imposter, isolate them and cut them off. Likewise, I have to identify which sound comes from my Heavenly Father and make sure that sound is amplified in my life so that it drowns out all others.

> *"The Spirit you received does not make you slaves, so that you live in fear again; rather, the Spirit you received brought about your adoption to son ship. And by Him we cry, 'Abba, Father." (Romans 8:15)*

Romans 8 identifies two spirits – the spirit of fear and the Spirit of God. Each of these spirits results in an identity. The spirit of fear produces slaves; the Spirit of God produces sons.

Whichever voice is the dominating sound in my life will result in my identity. If fear and all its other brothers and sisters (condemnation, guilt, accusation etc.) become the dominating sound in my life, the result is that I will become a slave.

However, there is a competing sound – the sound of the Holy Spirit. When I reject the sound of fear, and I amplify the sound of the Holy Spirit in my life, the Holy Spirit acts to fear like what kryptonite did to superman! Its chains are broken over my life and my identity becomes that of a child of God.

Notice that these two identities cannot co-exist. I am either a slave or a son. But I cannot be both. I can either choose to listen to the imposter or I can choose to listen to God. I can either believe what the enemy says about me or I can believe what God says about me.

Here is what God says about you:

- I am God's child. (Galatians 3:26)

- I am Jesus' friend. (John 15:15)

- I am a whole new person with a whole new life. (2 Corinthians 5:17)

- I am a place where God's Spirit lives. (1 Corinthians 6:19)

- I am God's incredible work of art (Ephesians 2:10)

- I am totally and completely forgiven (1 John 1:9)

- I am created in God's likeness (Ephesians 4:24)

- I am spiritually alive. (Ephesians 2:5)

- I am a citizen of Heaven. (Philippians 3:20)

- I am God's messenger to the world. (Acts 1:8)

- I am God's disciple-maker. (Matthew 28:19)

- I am the salt of the earth. (Matthew 5:13)

- I am the light of the world. (Matthew 5:14)

- I am greatly loved. (Romans 5:8)

We have to make a decision today –

I will not listen to the voice of my past. I will not listen to the voices of shame, condemnation, guilt or unworthiness. I will not listen to fear. I am not a slave or an orphan. I am a child of God. I am who my Father says I am. All other voices I identity as the voice of an imposter and I reject them. I hold on to the voice of truth which is the voice of my Father.

Only knowing the truth shall set us free (John 8:32). Truth has a sound – it is the voice of God.

## **Living Stillness**

The prophet Elijah was a man who was accustomed to hearing the voice of God, but one day he allowed the voice of an imposter to speak into his life.

*"Jezebel sent a messenger to Elijah to say, 'May the gods deal with me, be it ever so severely, if by this time tomorrow I do not make your life like that of one of them."*
*(1 Kings 19:2)*

Jezebel hijacked the speaker system of Elijah's life and her words acted like poison, resulting in Elijah being filled with so much fear that he ran for his life. As we read the account, Elijah goes on to suffer from exhaustion and depression, leading to suicidal thoughts. This is the devastating consequence that can come from listening to the wrong sound.

But what is God's fix for his suicidal servant?

> *"After the fire came a gentle whisper. When Elijah heard it, he pulled his cloak over his face and went out and stood at the mouth of the cave. Then a voice said to him, 'What are you doing here, Elijah?" (v12-13)*

kol demama daka – translated in English as "a gentle whisper" or a "still small voice". Actually, this an inadequate translation. In Hebrew the phrase is more accurately translated as "the sound of a thin silence". Perhaps the English translators translated it the way they did because it doesn't seem to make any sense; how can silence have a sound? But those who have been alone with God are accustomed to the 'kol demama daka' of His presence – the sound of a thin silence or a soft murmuring sound. It is living stillness – a sound that you can only hear if you are really listening. God's solution is to take Elijah away from every noise, every distraction, and there in the stillness, in the silence, God speaks. The Good Shepherd speaks. The voice of truth. The voice of Abba.

In the silence, the sound of Abba is louder and more powerful than the shout of the enemy. Many of us need a 'kol demama daka' moment. The noise of the wind, the noise of the fire and the earthquake were certainly spectacular, but it was in the silence that Elijah heard the sound of heaven and it was only that that he responded to.

Sometimes we have to just get alone with God. We have to tune out the noise of the world, the noise of people's opinion, the noise of the news, the noise of every distraction, even the internal noise that doesn't find its source from God's word. It is there in the desert, in the mouth of the cave, alone with God, in the silence that heaven speaks – affirming who we are and who we belong to.

### Did He mean it?

The crucifixion was certainly not a quiet affair. As the crowds gathered on Golgotha there were the sounds of men dying in agony. But eventually above the sounds of tears and groans, came a sound that drowned out them all, the sound of the Son of God crying, "It is finished!"

This sound was not the cry of a defeated man, but it was the cry of victory! Jesus had done it! He had ended the curse, defeated the enemy, made a new covenant in His blood and paid the price so that mankind could be forgiven, free, live forever and be adopted into sonship.

A few nights ago, my four year old son Judah and I were reading together the story of the crucifixion. As I put him to bed, Judah turned and said, "Daddy, did Jesus get it wrong?" Confused, I asked what he meant. "When he said, 'It is finished' did he get it wrong?" Now I was even more confused. "What do you mean, son?" "Well, there are lots of sick and broken people in the world, so did Jesus get it wrong when he said, 'it is finished'?" Pausing for a moment to think I replied, "No Judah. When Jesus said, 'It is finished', he really meant it. All the bad things in the world were defeated. Sadly, not everyone believes in what Jesus said and has received it."

Closing his bedroom door, I felt God speak to me. "Well, what about you? Do you believe it? Do you believe I meant it when I said, 'It is finished?' Do you believe it when I said, 'You are forgiven'? Do you believe it when I said, 'You are healed'? Do you believe it when I said that I called you and chose you?"

I felt challenged again in my spirit. Whose voice would I believe? Who would I listen to? The voice of the imposter or the voice of Truth. Jesus really did mean it when He said, "It is finished". He really did mean every promise He has spoken over our lives. He really did mean it when he said we are God's children and He lives within us always.

I choose today to turn off the voice of the imposter and to amplify the voice from the cross that two thousand years later still declares, "I have done it all. The victory is mine. It is finished!" Only that voice matters!

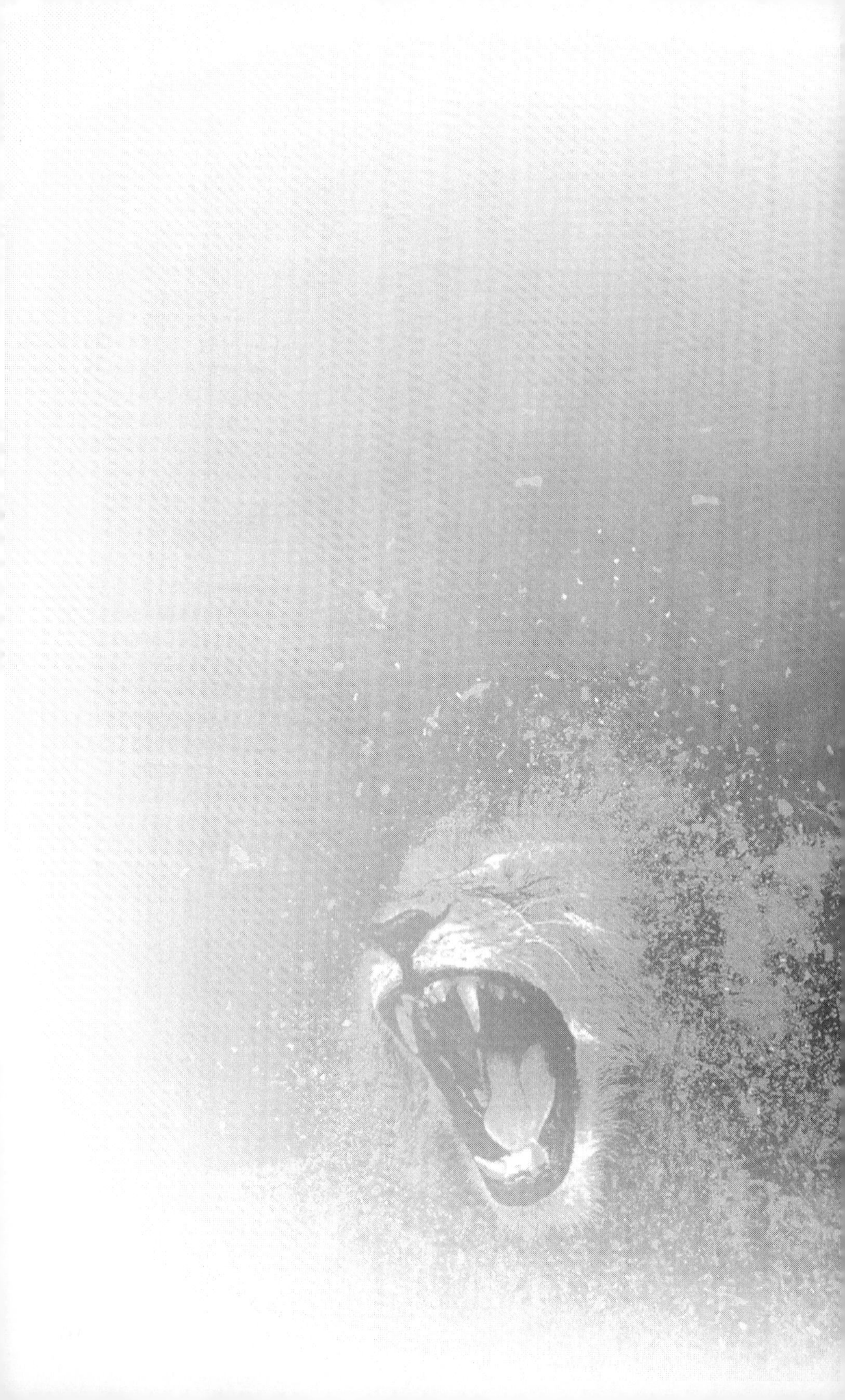

# THE SOUND OF BLOOD

*"Jesus the mediator of a new covenant, and to the sprinkled blood that speaks a better word than the blood of Abel." (Hebrews 12:24)*

Genesis 4 tells us the story of two brothers. After the beauty and wonder of the creation account and the tragedy of the fall, the narrative quickly switches to tell us this story of treachery, violence and murder.

Cain and Abel, sons of Adam and Eve, both decide to give an offering to God. Cain's offering which came out of the produce of the land is rejected by God, whereas Abel's offering, that of a lamb, is found pleasing in God's eyes.

Consumed with jealousy and anger, Cain tricks his brother into going out in the field where he "attacked his brother Abel and killed him" (Genesis 4:8).

Thinking he had got away with this despicable act, Cain tries to deny any knowledge of Abel's whereabouts when confronted by God.

But what Cain doesn't know is that there is a witness to what he has done. The witness may be soaked into the dirt, but nevertheless it speaks to God about what has happened.

"The Lord said, 'What have you done? Listen! Your brother's blood cries out to Me from the ground." (Genesis 4:10)

This is the first time the Bible states something that will become a major truth of the Scriptures – blood has a sound.

Even though Cain thought that he had ended his brother's life, Abel's blood still contained within it a sound that spoke to God.

The writer to Hebrews tells us that thousands of years later Abel "still speaks, even though he is dead" (Hebrews 11:4).

## The blood speaks

Leviticus 17:11 reveals to us that "the life of a creature is in the blood". This is a great mystery, but God is indicating that blood is sacred. Blood has a voice. Blood has a language. It seems that this sound is eternal – it never stops speaking to God.

Even though the breath of life had departed from Abel's body, the life in his blood still spoke to God. The blood cried out for revenge; the blood cried out for justice to be done.

The idea of blood having a sound that speaks to God is something that we see throughout the pages of the Bible.

In the book of Exodus, the final plague that falls on the Egyptians is the death of the first-born son. God instructed His people to take the blood of a lamb and apply it to the doorframes of their houses.

*"On that same night I will pass through Egypt and strike down every firstborn of both people and animals, and I will bring judgment on all the gods of Egypt. I am the Lord. The blood will be a sign for you on the houses where you are, and when I see the blood, I will pass over you. No destructive plague will touch you when I strike Egypt." (Exodus 12:12-13)*

When the angel of death came to the homes of the Israelites, he passed them over and their children lived. Why? Because the blood spoke on their behalf. The blood testified as to who they were and who they belonged to. Whereas the houses of the Egyptians were filled with the sounds of weeping and wailing (v30), no such fate came to the Israelites. The blood spoke for them and resulted in their salvation and deliverance.

Throughout the rest of the writings of Moses, the Bible goes into great detail describing all the various sacrifices and offerings that God's people had to make. Many of these sacrifices were blood sacrifices. The Old Testament tells us of the power of these sacrifices. The blood of the animals that were killed spoke to God on their behalf. The sound of the blood was heard by God and brought about atonement and forgiveness.

But all of these sacrifices and offerings were just a picture, just a foretaste, just a foreshadowing of the ultimate sacrifice, and the ultimate offering. They were all pointing to Jesus, "the Lamb of God, who takes away the sin of the world!" (John 1:29).

As Abel was the son of Adam, Jesus was the son of God. As Abel offered a lamb, Jesus became the lamb. As Abel's life was taken from him, Jesus laid down His life.

As Abel's blood cried out to God, so the blood of Jesus cries out to God too.

The New Testament tells us that the blood of Jesus "speaks a better word than the blood of Abel" (Hebrews 12:24).

The blood of Abel cried out for revenge; the blood of Jesus declares forgiveness. The blood of Abel cried out for justice to be done, the blood of Jesus declares that justice has been done. All of God's wrath and anger at sin has been fully satisfied in the death of His Son.

The blood of Jesus speaks to God on our behalf. It speaks a better word. The sound of the blood of Jesus is one of mercy, grace and salvation.

The sound of His blood is the sound of atonement:

*"For this reason, He had to be made like them, fully human in every way, in order that He might become a merciful and faithful high priest in service to God, and that He might make atonement for the sins of the people." (Hebrews 2:17)*

The sound of His blood is the sound of forgiveness:

*"Without the shedding of blood there is no forgiveness." (Hebrews 9:22)*

The sound of His blood is the sound of justification:

*"Since we have now been justified by His blood, how much more shall we be saved from God's wrath through Him!" (Romans 5:9)*

The sound of His blood is the sound of cleansing:

*"The law requires that nearly everything be cleansed with blood" (Hebrews 9:22).*

The sound of His blood is the sound of righteousness:

*"God made Him who had no sin to be sin for us, so that in Him we might become the righteousness of God." (2 Corinthians 5:21)*

The sound of His blood is the sound of redemption:

*"For you know that it was not with perishable things such as silver or gold that you were redeemed from the empty way of life handed down to you from your ancestors, but with the precious blood of Christ, a lamb without blemish or defect." (1 Peter 1:18-19)*

The sound of His blood is the sound that our sin has been done away with:

*"For Christ did not enter a sanctuary made with human hands that was only a copy of the true one; He entered heaven itself, now to appear for us in God's presence. Nor did He enter heaven to offer Himself again and again, the way the high priest enters the Most Holy Place every year with blood that is not his own. Otherwise Christ would have had to suffer many times since the creation of the world. But He has appeared once for all at the culmination of the ages to do away with sin by the sacrifice of Himself." (Hebrews 9:24-26)*

The sound of His blood is that which testifies that we are holy:

*"And so, Jesus also suffered outside the city gate to make the people holy through His own blood." (Hebrews 13:12)*

The sound of His blood is that which testifies that we have been made perfect:

*"For by one sacrifice He has made perfect for ever those who are being made holy." (Hebrews 10:14)*

The sound of His blood is the signal that we can draw near to God:

*"But now in Christ Jesus you who once were far away have been brought near by the blood of Christ" (Ephesians 2:13).*

The sound of His blood is that which testifies that we have peace with God:

*"For God was pleased to have all His fullness dwell in Him, and through Him to reconcile to Himself all things, whether things on earth or things in heaven, by making peace through His blood, shed on the cross." (Colossians 1:19-20)*

The sound of His blood is what our confidence is in:

*"We have confidence to enter the Most Holy Place by the blood of Jesus" (Hebrews 10:19).*

The sound of His blood is the sound of victory:

> "They triumphed over him by the blood of the Lamb and by the word of their testimony" (Revelation 12:11).

The sound of His blood is our life:

> "Whoever eats my flesh and drinks my blood has eternal life, and I will raise them up at the last day." (John 6:54)

The sound of His blood signals a new covenant has been made:

> "This is My blood of the covenant, which is poured out for many for the forgiveness of sins." (Matthew 26:28)

The sound of His blood is the promise of our resurrection:

> "The God of peace, who through the blood of the eternal covenant brought back from the dead our Lord Jesus" (Hebrews 13:20).

## **Judah and Tamar**

Genesis 38 is one of the strangest chapters in the Bible. Missing out some of the more salacious details, let me give you a brief overview of the story of Judah and Tamar.

Tamar is the daughter-in-law of Judah, wife of his first-born son Er. Er dies leaving Tamar as a childless widow. Because of the custom of the day, Judah is obliged to giver Tamar to his second oldest son Onan, so that Tamar can have children with him and not live with the disgrace of being childless. But Onan also dies and once again Tamar is left as a widow.

Judah refuses to give Tamar his next oldest son Shelah and so she is faced with a desperate choice to make.

Tamar dresses as a prostitute and Judah, not realising that it his daughter-in-law (she would have worn a veil), sleeps with her. Because he has no means of payment on hand, he leaves behind with Tamar three items at her request – his seal and its cord and his staff as a pledge of future payment.
Let us pick up the story from verse 24:

*"About three months later Judah was told, 'Your daughter-in-law Tamar is guilty of prostitution, and as a result she is now pregnant.'*
*Judah said, 'Bring her out and let her be burned to death!'*

*As she was being brought out, she sent a message to her father-in-law. 'I am pregnant by the man who owns these,' she said. And she added, 'See if you recognise whose seal and cord and staff these are.'*

*Judah recognised them and said, 'She is more righteous than I, since I wouldn't give her to my son Shelah.' And he did not sleep with her again." (v24-26)*

You can imagine the fear as Tamar first discovers she is pregnant. Perhaps hiding her pregnancy at first, she reaches the moment when it becomes obvious to all. She knows that what she has done will be discovered and certain death awaits her.

But Tamar has three things – the staff, the cord, the seal. She has hidden them in a safe place. She knows that her life depends on Judah recognising them. It is her only way of escape. She puts all of her hope in those three items. She trusts that what they speak will be enough to save her.

Finally, the day comes when Judah demands she is burnt at the stake. In that moment Tamar knows her time has come. Showing Judah the staff, the cord, the seal she asks one question of her father-in-law – who do these belong to?

Realisation hits Judah. It is his staff, his cord, his seal. These three items speak for her, they prove her innocence and his guilt. Not only does he spare her her life, but he actually declares her righteous.

What has this to do with us? Like Tamar we have all broken God's laws and are deserving of death, deserving of the fires of hell. We have no excuses; our guilt is obvious.

But we have a message we can deliver to the Father. We have three things that we have put all of our hope in, all of our confidence in. Our eternal destiny depends on these things speaking for us.

The staff of authority speaks of the Name of Jesus – *"Salvation is found in no one else, for there is no other name under heaven given to mankind by which we must be saved." (Acts 4:12)*

The cord speaks of the precious blood of Jesus *"that speaks a better word than the blood of Abel." (Hebrews 12:24)*

The seal speaks of the Holy Spirit, our Advocate – "When the Advocate comes, whom I will send to you from the Father – the Spirit of truth who goes out from the Father – He will testify about Me." (John 15:26)

As we stand before the Father, aware of our guilt and our shame, what is our only defence? Whose Name is it that I have trusted in? Whose blood has cleansed me? Whose Spirit lives in me?

The Name, the blood, the Spirit – they speak to the Father on our behalf. They are our hope and plea. They are the greatest lawyers we could ever hope for.

The Father recognises the Name – it is the Name of His Son. He recognises the blood – it is the blood of His Son. The Father recognises the Spirit – it is the Spirit of His Son.

The Name, the blood, the Spirit – they testify for us. As the Father listens to them, He has no choice but to declare us innocent and to pronounce righteousness over us.

## The accuser is silenced

The name Satan means "the accuser" and this is one of his roles. Satan accuses us before God, saying why we are unworthy and undeserving of salvation. Many times, we hear the voice of the accuser speaking into our own lives, reminding us of our past, reminding us of our failures.

In John 8, a woman caught in adultery is brought before Jesus. All around her are the accusers, demanding that Jesus condemn this woman:

> *Jesus bent down and started to write on the ground with His finger. When they kept on questioning Him, He straightened up and said to them, 'Let any one of you who is without sin be the first to throw a stone at her.' Again He stooped down*

> *and wrote on the ground.*
> *At this, those who heard began to go away one at a time, the older ones first, until only Jesus was left, with the woman still standing there. Jesus straightened up and asked her, 'Woman, where are they? Has no one condemned you?'*
> *'No one, sir,' she said.*
> *'Then neither do I condemn you,' Jesus declared. 'Go now and leave your life of sin.' (v7-11)*

In the eyes of the law this woman was guilty. In the eyes of God this woman was guilty. The accuser had every right to declare how sinful she was.

And yet faced with the sound of the accuser, Jesus stood silent. Jesus' silence spoke louder than their accusation.

Why did Jesus not condemn this woman? The hypocrisy of the accusers was obvious, but Jesus was the One without sin, He could have thrown the stones.

Perhaps Jesus was looking ahead to a short time after this when He would go to the cross and shed His blood.

He knew that His blood would make a sound that would drown out her sin, drown out her guilt, drown out her shame.

No matter what we have done, no matter how great our sin – His blood silences the accuser, His blood silences guilt and shame. His blood turns off the reminder of our past. His blood defends us, justifies us, declares us "not guilty"

> "My dear children, I write this to you so that you will not sin. But if anybody does sin, we have an advocate with the Father – Jesus Christ, the Righteous One."
> (1 John 2:1)

> "Then he showed me Joshua the high priest standing before the angel of the Lord, and Satan standing at his right side to accuse him. The Lord said to Satan, 'The Lord rebuke you, Satan! The Lord, who has chosen Jerusalem, rebuke you! Is not this man a burning stick snatched from the fire?'
> Now Joshua was dressed in filthy clothes as he stood before the angel. The angel said to those who were standing before him, 'Take off his filthy clothes.'
> Then he said to Joshua, 'See, I have taken away your sin, and I will put fine garments on you.'
> Then I said, 'Put a clean turban on his head.' So they put a clean turban on his head and clothed him, while the angel of the Lord stood by." (Zechariah 3:1-5)

In the courtroom of heaven, God refuses to listen to the accuser. He chooses to be deaf towards the law that speaks against you. Your defender, your advocate speaks on your behalf and that is what the Father hears. Your advocates evidence is His own blood, shed for you. It speaks louder than your past, louder than your shame, louder than your mistakes – it rebukes the accuser, declares you innocent and clean.

Isaiah 53 tells us of what Jesus went through on the cross:

> "Surely, he took up our pain and bore our suffering, yet we considered him punished by God, stricken by him, and afflicted. But he was pierced for our transgressions, he was crushed for our iniquities; the punishment that brought us peace was on him, and by his wounds we are healed.

*We all, like sheep, have gone astray, each of us has turned to our own way; and the Lord has laid on him the iniquity of us all. He was oppressed and afflicted, yet he did not open his mouth; he was led like a lamb to the slaughter, and as a sheep before its shearers is silent, so he did not open his mouth." (Isaiah 53:4-7)*

In the face of such pain and agony, Jesus chose to be silent. He did not defend Himself; He chose to let His blood do the talking. Now that blood speaks on your behalf. That blood testifies that your sins are forgiven, that blood testifies of your peace, that blood testifies that your wounds have been healed.

The word 'pain' in verse 4, is the Hebrew word that means "illness, sickness, affliction or wound". This speaks of the price for physical healing that was payed for through His blood.

The blood speaks louder than all sickness, all disease, all pain or all diagnosis of doctors. Show your sickness His wounds. His wounds speak healing, His wounds speak wholeness, His wounds speak restoration of health and life.

## Communion

I want to share with you some thoughts from my previous book "The Miracle Table: Rediscovering the Power of Communion"

According to Jesus, the act of Communion is an act of proclamation: "you proclaim the Lord's death until He comes" (1 Corinthians 11:26). What are we proclaiming?

We are proclaiming that another decree has been made. Satan may have pronounced death over us, but the King has made another decree: "death is defeated". Satan may have pronounced sickness over us, but the King makes another decree: "by My stripes you are healed". God does not ignore our sins and failures, but in response to the accuser He makes another decree: "My blood cleanses, My blood forgives, My blood washes away, My blood makes you clean, My blood makes you righteous, My blood makes you worthy". Glory to God, that the words of this second decree, the power of this New Covenant are more powerful than the words of the written code that has been nailed to the tree with Him. Those words now no longer have power over us: "All sins forgiven, the slate wiped clean, that old arrest warrant cancelled and nailed to Christ's cross" (Colossians 2:14 - The Message).

The Bread and the Wine have a language and a voice.

For us today, the Bread and the Wine still speak. Even though the body of Christ was broken two thousand years ago, His sacrifice still speaks, His wounds still speak. They still speak of our salvation; they still speak of our healing. Even now in the presence of God our King, the blood of Christ is still speaking on our behalf. There is still life in His blood, His blood still speaks. It speaks to God for us and enables us to be brought into the throne room of Heaven and the presence of the King of kings. We have access because the blood testifies on our behalf. It speaks mercy, grace, and acceptance.

## **Nothing But The Blood**

Guilt, shame and unworthiness are toxic and will surely lead to a life of defeat. This is why satan comes as the accuser, reminding us of our past and our failures.

But remember today that the blood of Jesus has a sound. The blood of Jesus speaks: His blood testifies that we are God's children; His blood testifies that we are forgiven; His blood testifies that we have been made righteous.

The sound of His blood is louder than the sound of the accuser. God chooses to be deaf towards the voice of the accuser and He chooses to listen to the sound of Jesus' blood. He no longer hears our sin or our past. They have gone, they have been removed. The blood has spoken in our defence and our behalf and declared us "not guilty".

> Your blood speaks a better word
> Than all the empty claims I've heard upon this earth
> Speaks righteousness for me
> And stands in my defence
> Jesus, it's Your blood
> Your blood
>
> Your blood speaks a better word
> Than all the empty claims I've heard upon this earth
> Speaks righteousness for me
> And stands in my defence
> Jesus, it's Your blood
>
> What can wash away our sins?
> What can make us whole again?
> Nothing but the blood
> Nothing but the blood of Jesus
> What can wash us pure as snow
> Welcomed as the friends of God?
> Nothing but Your blood
> Nothing but Your blood, King Jesus

Your cross testifies in grace
Tells of the Father's heart to make a way for us
Now boldly we approach
Not earthy confidence
It's only by Your blood

What can wash away our sins?
What can make us whole again?
Nothing but the blood
Nothing but the blood of Jesus
What can wash us pure as snow
Welcomed as the friends of God?
Nothing but Your blood
Nothing but Your blood, King Jesus

© Matt Redman


The blood of Jesus speaks for me
Be still my soul, redeeming love
Out of the dust of Calvary
Is rising to the throne above
There is no vengeance in His cry
While 'It is finished' fills the sky
forgiveness is the final plea
The blood of Jesus speaks for me

When my accuser makes the claim
That I should die for my offense

I point him to that rugged frame
Where I found life at Christ's expense
See from His hands, His feet, His side
The fountain flowing deep and wide
Oh, He did shout the victory
The blood of Jesus speaks for me

Oh, let my soul arise and sing
My confidence is not in vain
The one who fights for me is King
His hope, His covenant remain
No condemnation now I dread
Eternal hope is mine instead
His word will stand, I stand redeemed
The blood of Jesus speaks for me

© Travis Cottrell

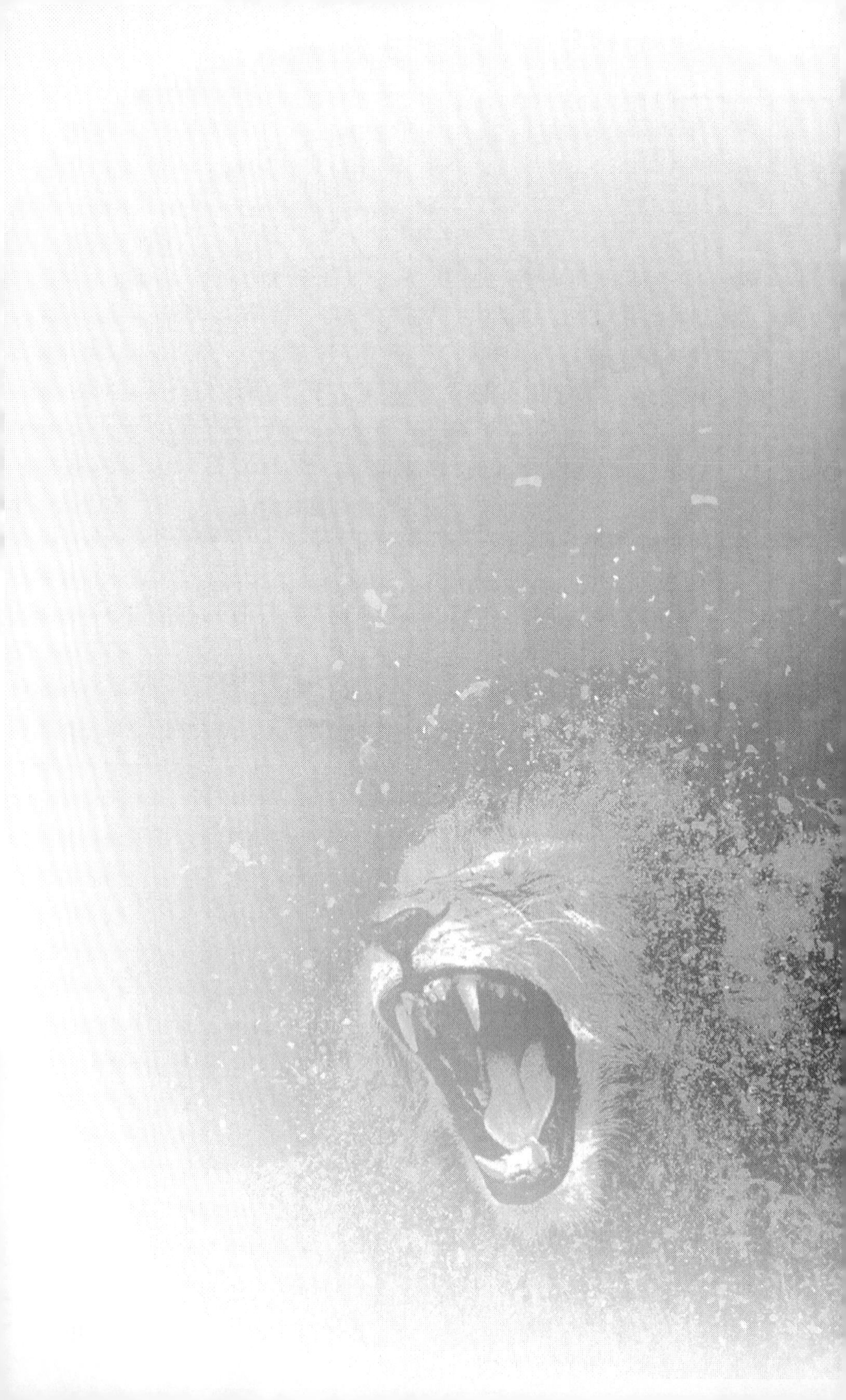

# THE SOUND OF PASSION

*"When he heard that it was Jesus of Nazareth, he began to shout" (Mark 10:47)*

In this chapter we are going to go into the gospels and read about one of my favourite Bible characters: a blind beggar called Bartimaeus. I want to you to read with me his story as found in Mark chapter 10.

*"Then they came to Jericho. As Jesus and His disciples, together with a large crowd, were leaving the city, a blind man, Bartimaeus (which means 'son of Timaeus'), was sitting by the roadside begging. When he heard that it was Jesus of Nazareth, he began to shout, 'Jesus, Son of David, have mercy on me!'*
*Many rebuked him and told him to be quiet, but he shouted all the more, 'Son of David, have mercy on me!'*
*Jesus stopped and said, 'Call him.'*
*So they called to the blind man, 'Cheer up! On your feet! He's calling you.'*
*Throwing his cloak aside, he jumped to his feet and came to Jesus.*
*'What do you want me to do for you?' Jesus asked him.*
*The blind man said, 'Rabbi, I want to see.'*
*'Go,' said Jesus, 'your faith has healed you.' Immediately he received his sight and followed Jesus along the road." (Mark 10:47-52)*

As we read about this man there are of course many things that we don't know about him. We don't know what he looked like. We don't know how old he was. We don't know his marital status. But there are three things that we do know about him – firstly that he was blind, secondly that he was a beggar and thirdly we know that his name was Bartimaeus. Now let's just pause there for a moment.

How many people in the New Testament did Jesus heal? The answer – a lot! Has it ever struck you that the gospel writers never tell us the name of anyone that Jesus healed? We know them by their condition – the paralysed man, the woman with the issue of blood, the man with leprosy – but we don't know any of their names (I am not including Lazarus who was raised from the dead). In fact the only time when Jesus heals someone and it gives you their name is this one time – the blind man, Bartimaeus. Now maybe that is just coincidental or maybe the Holy Spirit wants to draw our attention to something significant about this man's name.

## What's in a name?

When Jewish parents named their children, they didn't just pick a name at random. For them it was an incredibly significant and spiritual act. Jewish tradition even states that when a child is born, an angel will come and whisper to the parents what that child will be called. The naming of a child was a prophetic act – the parents were prophesying who that child would be and what they would become.

So what does the name Bartimaeus mean? The first part "Bar" simply means "Son of". The second part "Timaeus" means "honour". So the name "Bartimaeus" means "The Son of Honour".

I want you to imagine the scene as the proud parents gathered their friends and neighbours round about them. No doubt they were all keen to know what this new-born baby would be called. Timaeus, with his arm around his wife, looks proudly at his new-born son and says, "I name him 'The Son of Honour'. I declare over his life that when he grows up people will honour him, people will respect him. He will live a life of dignity. Everyone in Jericho will come to honour my son".

Now we fast-forward – 10 years, 20 years, we are unsure of the date – but where do we find the son of honour? Blind and begging and sat by the side of the road. Can anyone think of a less honourable situation than that? When was the last time anyone had called him by his name? Did anyone even know his name? Surely he was just known as "the blind man" or "the blind beggar". That was his reputation. His identity as a son of honour had long been forgotten.

What has that to do with you and me? Do you ever find yourself in life in a place where what your Father has spoken over you doesn't match up with your circumstances?

The Bible is more than just a list of rules and commandments. It is more than just stories. The Bible is a book full of prophetic declarations that your Father in Heaven has made over your life. Contained within its pages, your Father declares over you that you are healed, that you are free, that you are righteous, that He is your provider, that you are blessed, that you have joy. We could go on and on!

But do you ever find yourself like Bartimaeus? What the Father has spoken over you doesn't match up with your reality. The Father declares that you are healed, but you are sick. The Father declares that you are free, but you are bound. The Father declares that you are blessed, but you see no sign of blessing. You get the idea?

What do you do when you are called the son of honour, but you are begging by the side of the road? What do you do when you what the Father has spoken over you doesn't match up with your circumstances? You need an encounter with Jesus!

The good news for Bartimaeus that day was that Jesus had come to town! Why did Jesus visit Jericho that day? To heal a blind man? Yes, but more than that. He came to restore a man's identity. Never again would he be known as the blind man or the beggar. From this day on, he would be known as Bartimaeus, the son of honour. Jesus restored back to this man who his father had already declared that he was.

Two thousand years ago, Jesus entered my Jericho. He entered your Jericho. In the Old Testament, Jericho was a place cursed by God. On the cross, Jesus took the curse of our sin. Why? So that all that the Father declared over us could be a reality. Jesus made healing a reality, He made sonship a reality, He made freedom a reality. Jesus took our curse so that our identity could be restored and we could be all who God intended us to be.

## The sound of Jesus

For Bartimaeus that day began just like any other day as he was placed in his usual spot by the side of the road. All he was expecting as he felt the sun shine down was maybe a few shekels that would enable him to get through till the next day.

As he sat there, Bartimaeus began to listen to the usual sounds. Blind people are often more sensitive to sound than people with regular vision so perhaps he could overhear the conversations of market traders, he could hear the laughter of children, he could hear the bark of dogs.

But then the sound began to change and he began to hear a new sound. Mark tell us that he "heard that it was Jesus of Nazareth". Of course he couldn't see him, but he could hear him. He could hear the sound of the presence of Jesus. Just like Adam all those years ago, he could hear the sound of God Himself walking by.

We don't know what it was that Bartimaeus heard but there was something in that sound that caused a response in Bartimaeus.

It is a truth that many times before you see Jesus, you will hear Him. Before you see the manifestation you will hear a sound.

Revival, the miraculous, an encounter with God – they all contain a unique sound and often you will hear that sound before you will see the actual breakthrough. It is how you respond to what you can hear that will determine whether you will actually get to see it!

Mark's gospel actually contains several accounts of people hearing about Jesus before they saw him.

Mark 2 tells us that people heard that Jesus had come to Capernaum and in response gathered to listen to His teaching. So many that they couldn't all fit in the house! (Mark 2:1-2).

Mark 3 tells us that large crowds heard about all the miracles that Jesus was doing and pushed forward to be healed of their diseases (Mark 3:8).

Mark 5 tells us that a woman with an issue of blood, heard all about Jesus and her response was to push through a crowd of people to get her healing (Mark 5:27).

Mark 6 tells us that many who heard His teaching were amazed (Mark 6:2).

Later in the same chapter, we read that wherever people heard that He was, they brought the sick to Him (Mark 6:55).

Mark 7 tells us about a woman, whose daughter had a demon, hearing about Jesus and in response crying out to Him for a miracle (Mark 7:25).

Before any of these people met Jesus, they heard Him. They heard the sound of His presence. They heard the sound of who He was and what He could do.

The sound of His presence carried with it hope and expectancy. Sometimes a sound is more than a sound. Have you ever been to a rock concert and stood next to a speaker? You don't just hear the sound, you can feel it! The sound contains more than just noise. The sound of His presence is pregnant with the miraculous, pregnant with possibility.

As they heard heaven's sound, all of these people responded. Whether it was to run to Him, touch Him or cry out to Him, they knew that they had to respond when they heard the sound of His presence.

It was as they responded to the sound of His presence that they got to see His presence! Then their testimony could be the same as that of the Samaritan village to the woman at the well:

> "We no longer believe just because of what you said; now we have heard for ourselves, and we know that this man really is the Saviour of the world." (John 6:42)

## Bartimaeus' response

So how did Bartimaeus respond to the sound of Jesus passing by? The Bible tells us that he made his own sound – he began to shout!

Trying desperately to make his voice heard over the crowds that were gathered around Jesus, he opened his mouth and began to shout as loud as he could "Jesus, son of David have mercy on me!"

It was the sound of passion. It was the sound of desperation. It was the sound of faith. It was the sound of need crying out to the miracle worker.

Contained within that cry was this longing: "Jesus, don't pass me by!"

Read the passage again and note that Jesus was actually leaving Jericho. The sound of Jesus that Bartimaeus could hear was actually moving away from him. He could hear the footsteps of Jesus walking past him; he could hear the sound of the crowd getting fainter. God was passing him by and he had yet to receive his miracle.

Something rose up within Bartimaeus in that moment. He would not let Jesus pass him by. He would not allow the Healer to leave his town without him receiving his breakthrough. He had to do something before it was too late. There was an urgency in his spirit. This was his time. This was his moment.

It would have been so easy for Bartimaeus to have just sat there and enjoyed the presence of Jesus for those few brief moments. It would have been a great story to tell! "The Day Jesus Walked By!" He could have describe the sound in detail. He could have talked about the goose-bumps and the emotion that he felt. But he would still have been blind!

Bartimaeus knew that a brief moment in Jesus' presence was not enough. He needed a face to face encounter. Only seeing Jesus would change his circumstances.

Many times we sit in church and we enjoy the presence of Jesus. We enjoy the peace. We enjoy the atmosphere. We hear the sounds of praise and worship. We hear the sound of the Bible being taught. And it's all good – but we never change. We come in bound, we leave bound; we come in sick, we leave sick; we come in broken, we leave broken.

Only seeing Him, experiencing Him, touching Him. Only that changes us. Only a face to face encounter with God will transform us and our circumstances.

God is putting a sound back into His church. It is the sound of hunger; it is the sound of passion; it is the sound of desperation. No longer are we content just sitting passively while God moves but we remain untouched. We are crying out for a face to face encounter with God. We want to see His glory. This is our time. This is our moment. We have heard of His fame and His miracles but now we want to see them in our day (Habakkuk 3:2)

## The response of the crowd

What is remarkable is that on hearing the sound of Bartimaeus shout, many started to rebuke him. This wasn't just one or two grumpy people, the vast majority of the people in the crowd that day were offended by Bartimaeus' passion!

The devil is never concerned about you sitting in a seat in church. As long as you sit there passively, you don't bother him for a moment. But the moment you start to make a sound, the moment you begin to release a sound of passion, a sound of desperation, the moment you begin to cry out for a face to face encounter with Jesus, the moment you begin to cry out "something in my life has to change" – that is when you make satan very nervous.

The devil will do everything within his power to drown out your shout. He will send religious people, he will send controlling leadership, he will send sickness, doubt, unbelief and circumstances – anything he can to dull your passion, to drown out your shout.

But I love the response of Bartimaeus! As the crowd told him to stop shouting, he shouted even louder!

When the enemy shouts, you have to shout louder. When fear shouts, shout louder. When unbelief shouts, shout louder. When shame shouts, should louder. When religion shouts, shout louder!

As the song by Bethel music declares:

> I raise a hallelujah, in the presence of my enemies
> I raise a hallelujah, louder than the unbelief
> I raise a hallelujah, my weapon is a melody
> I raise a hallelujah, Heaven comes to fight for me
>
> I'm gonna sing, in the middle of the storm
> Louder and louder, you're gonna hear my praises roar
> Up from the ashes, hope will arise
> Death is defeated, the King is alive
>
> I raise a hallelujah, with everything inside of me
> I raise a hallelujah, I will watch the darkness flee
> I raise a hallelujah, in the middle of the mystery
> I raise a hallelujah, fear you lost your hold on me
>
> Sing a little louder
> In the presence of my enemies

Sing a little louder
Louder than the unbelief
Sing a little louder
My weapon is a melody
Sing a little louder
Heaven comes to fight for me

© Songwriters: Jonathan David Helser / Melissa Helser / Molly Skaggs / Jake Stevens
Raise a Hallelujah lyrics © Bethel Music Publishing

Is it just me that finds it fascinating that all of this took place in Jericho? What is the most famous event that happened in Jericho? In Joshua 6, the children of Israel come to Jericho, a walled city that stands between them and their promised land. God gives Joshua a unique strategy. March around the city for 6 days in complete silence. On the 7th day, march around the city 7 times. On the 7th time, blow a trumpet and "shout!"

"When the trumpets sounded, the army shouted, and at the sound of the trumpet, when the men gave a loud shout, the wall collapsed; so everyone charged straight in, and they took the city." (Joshua 6:20)

At the sound of the shout of God's people, the city walls fell and the children of Israel entered their destiny.

Now on the exact same piece of land, hundreds of years later, one blind beggar began to shout! As he did, the walls of his blindness and lack would collapse and he would enter into all that God had for him.

It was like there was a blocked well of encounter in that city that was waiting to be re-discovered and for a moment, as Bartimaeus raised his voice, he tapped into that anointing and saw heaven move in response. It was almost like the echo of Israel's shout was still lingering in the atmosphere of that town – and as Bartimaeus joined in with that shout, he got his own miracle.

I believe that the Church has been silent for too long. For too long we have been walking around the walls. For too long we have been sat by the side of the road. God is putting a shout back into His Church! God is restoring back to His Church a shout of praise, a cry of passion and a roar of victory!

For make no mistake, while the crowd was offended by Bartimaeus' passion, there was one person who was not offended – and it just so happened His was the only opinion that mattered!

I have read the Bible many times and never do I find a place where Jesus is offended by our passion! I can find no place where he rebukes someone for praying with too much faith or worshipping with too much passion! On the contrary, while He is never offended by our passion, He is always offended by our apathy.

You see, no one else in the crowd that day got their miracle. No one else in the crowd that day got their encounter. The breakthrough went to the shouting man! The miracle went to the desperate man!

## The response of Jesus

At the sound of Bartimaeus' shout, the Bible makes an extraordinary statement – "Jesus stopped".

These two words contain such power. Remember, Jesus is leaving town, He is heading out of Jericho. We know that Jesus never did anything or went anywhere by chance. He was always focused on His mission, always obeying His Father.

As far as Jesus was concerned, He had finished His assignment in Jericho. His job was done, He was moving on to the next place.

But a sound caused Him to stop in His tracks. A sound caused Him to turn back around. A sound caused Him to change direction. A sound moved Him.

What was it? It was the sound of a blind beggar who was desperate for a miracle. I am sure that there were lots of people in the crowd that day crying out to Jesus. There would have been lots of noise, lots of people shouting out. But there was something in the sound of Bartimaeus' shout that was different. There was something that Jesus heard that caught His attention. There was something that moved Him.

"Jesus, son of David, have mercy on me" – it is not the most profound, sophisticated prayer in the Bible. But Jesus heard something in the shout. He could hear the passion, He could hear the desperation, He could hear the faith. And it got heaven's attention. It moved the Son of God.

Passion has a sound. Hunger has a sound. Faith a sound. And they are irresistible to Jesus. He has to respond when He hears that sound.

Psalm 10:17 says *"You, Lord, hear the desire of the afflicted; You encourage them, and You listen to their cry"*

He doesn't just listen to your cry, He hears your desire. Even your desires have a sound that heaven responds to.

Can you image what happened as Jesus stopped? I can just picture everyone in the crowd stopping and a hush coming over them. What was wrong? What was He going to do?

Can you imagine Bartimaeus' thoughts as he listened to the scene? Suddenly all the noise around him had stopped. What on earth was going on?

Then in the middle of the silence he heard a voice. Did he know that it was the voice of Jesus? There must have been something in that voice that was different as he heard the words "Call him".

Bartimaeus waits. Who is this voice calling? Who is Jesus referring to? Then he feels someone shove him: "Cheer up, on your feet, He's calling you!"

Imagine the joy as Bartimaeus realises that the person being called is him! Surely there can be no greater sound than the sound of Jesus calling you: the sound that Jesus is calling you into a place of freedom and wholeness. Luke's account specifically tells us that Jesus ordered that Bartimaeus be brought near to Him (Luke 18:40). Ultimately this is the purpose of the sound of heaven. He calls us to Himself, His voice draws us into the nearness of His presence.

I find it amusing that it was the crowd that gave Bartimaeus the good news that Jesus was calling him. The same crowd that moments before had tried to silence him were now the same crowd that was bringing him to Jesus!

Here is the wonder of how God works! He will use the very thing that satan sent to silence you to be the very thing that He uses to bring you into His presence. Some of you would never have known the healer if it hadn't been for your sickness. You would never have known the deliverer if it hadn't been for your trial. You would never have known the provider if it wasn't for your need.

Satan sent cancer to silence you, he sent divorce to silence you, he sent addiction to silence you. But don't be silent. Don't let him rob you of your shout! Keep raising a sound of praise, a sound of victory, a sound of passion and watch as God uses the very thing the enemy sent to silence you be the very thing that He uses to bring you to Himself!

"Throwing His clock aside". This may seem like a throwaway line but it is very significant. Similar to a white stick today, in that culture, blind people were given a special cloak to wear that identified them as blind. So each day, as Bartimaeus was dressed, someone put on him a cloak that said: "This is who you are. This is your identity. This is who you will always be".

But that was not who Bartimaeus really was. At the sound of Jesus' call I don't know what Bartimaeus was thinking but maybe he was reminded of the sound of his parents' voice: "Son of honour, dinner is ready!" "Son of honour, have you tidied your room?" "Son of honour, it's time to get up!"

Something rose up within this blind beggar: "This is not who I am! I'm a son of honour! I refuse to wear the cloak another moment. I refuse to let this identify me. I am not the cloak – I am who my father says I am!"

Some of us have been defined by our past: we have been defined by a trauma or an abusive relationship, we have been defined by a disability or a diagnosis or an addiction. Some of us have been defined by what other people have spoken over us. We have worn these things like a cloak. They have become our identity.

But listen to the sound of Jesus' voice today. He is calling you. He is calling you into a place of wholeness. Listen to the sound of your Father's voice today. You are who He says you are. You are His child. You are not the cloak. You are a son of honour.

Like Bartimaeus, refuse to wear the cloak another second. Jesus will open your eyes, but you have to throw off the cloak. You have to make the decision today that you will no longer be defined by anything other than who He says you are.

Notice that as Bartimaeus made his way to Jesus he was still blind. How did he get to Jesus? He had to follow the sound of His voice. Sometimes all you have to go on is the sound of His voice. Sometimes all you have to go on is "I've heard Him call me". Even if you have to walk in the dark – keep following the sound of His voice. Even if you stumble once or twice – get up and keep following the sound of His voice. That voice will eventually lead you to His hand.

"Lord I want to see" – at the sound of that simple request, Jesus responded and Bartimaeus' eyes were opened. And the first thing he ever saw – the face of Jesus.

There is something about a face to face encounter with Jesus that changes everything. The Bible says that Bartimaeus followed Jesus down the road. Remember, Jesus was leaving town. Bartimaeus left his place at the side of the road, he left his beggars cloak, he left Jericho. And I believe that he never returned! I believe that it is more than likely that he joined Jesus' disciples and became a member of the early Church. In fact this is probably why we know his name.

Bartimaeus could have stayed passive that day when he heard Jesus pass by. But instead passion, hunger and desperation rose up within him and he created a sound that moved heaven. It would change his life forever.

Incidentally, it seems, looking at the timeline of Jesus' life, that He never visited Jericho again. If Bartimaeus had stayed silent that day, he would never have got his breakthrough.

Passivity is always the enemy of breakthrough. If today, in the presence of God, you can hear heaven's sound calling you then it's time to get desperate. It's time to create a sound of passion, a sound of hunger, a sound of faith. It's time to cry out for a face to face encounter with Jesus. We need to see His glory and be who He called us to be. The sound of that passion is a sound that heaven can't deny. Your passion moves Him. Who needs to know today - He is here and He is calling you? Let your shout be heard!

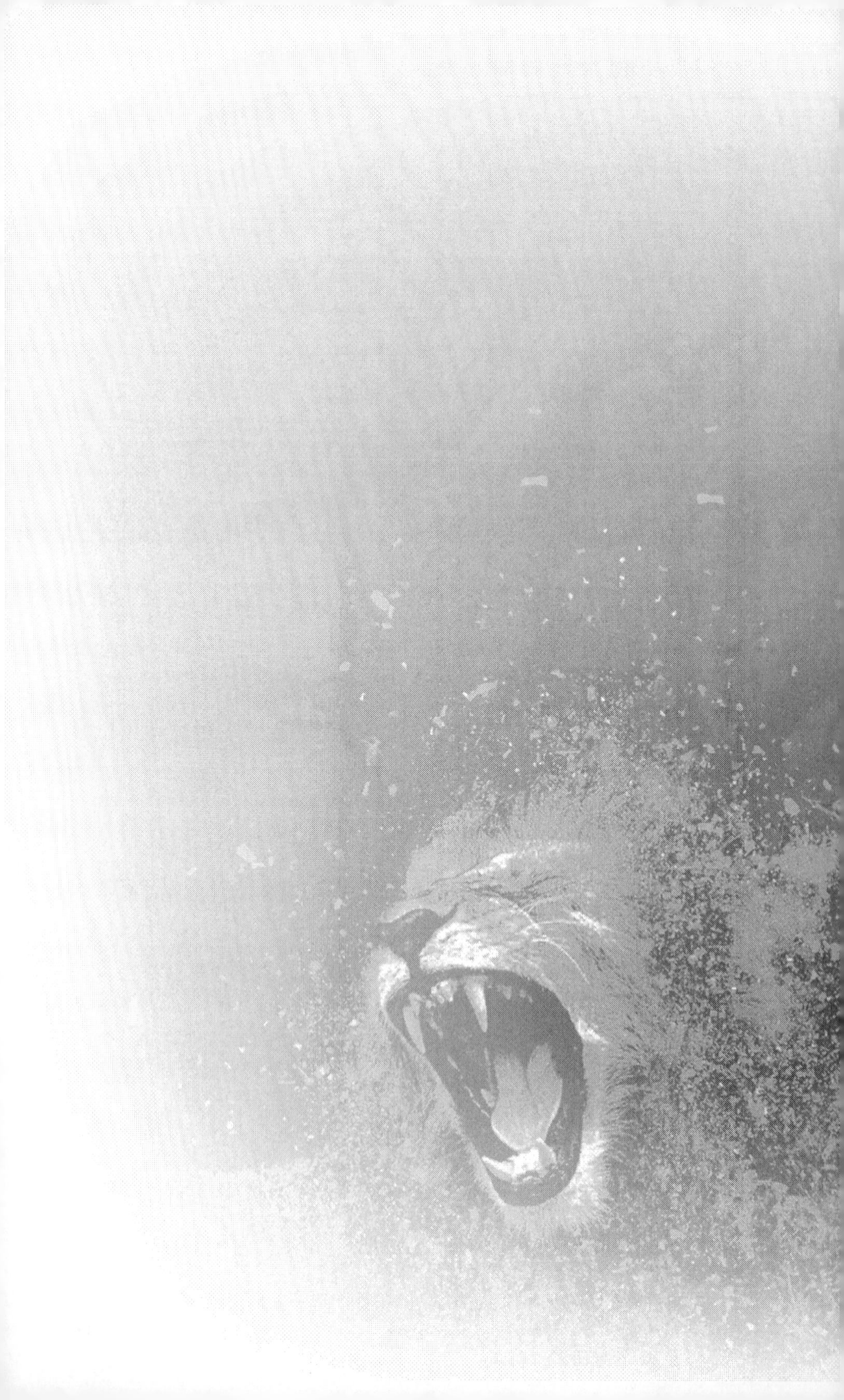

# THE SOUND OF PRAYER

*And as He taught them, He said, "Is it not written: 'My house will be called a house of prayer for all nations'? But you have made it 'a den of robbers.'" (Mark 11:17)*

As Jesus entered the temple with His disciples His ears were met by a sound that He didn't like. Expecting to hear people praying to God, instead Jesus heard the sound of trade as people bought and sold and exchanged money. This was not what God's house was meant to be. A righteous indignation rose up within Jesus and He began to overturn the tables and chase out those who were making God's temple a marketplace. Then Jesus made this statement: "My house will be called a house of prayer for all nations".

Jesus was establishing the priority and the focus of the temple – it was meant to be a place where the sound of prayer to God was heard. This priority of Jesus has not changed. Whether we speak of God's house as the Church, or our homes or each of us as individuals as the place where God lives, God expects His house to be a place of prayer. The sound of prayer should be found in our churches and our homes. We as individuals should be mobile houses of prayer, releasing the sounds of prayer wherever we go.

Make no mistake about it, God hears and answers prayer! 1 John 5:5 says, "This is the confidence we have in approaching God: that if we ask anything according to His will, He hears us." 1 Peter 3:12 tells us that "the eyes of the Lord are on the righteous and His ears are attentive to their prayer".

Both of these verses tell us this powerful truth – God hears my prayer! When I open my mouth and pray, God hears the sound of my voice and He responds. The power of the truth of prayer has somehow become lost in our culture. Yet think for a moment about this incredible reality: God Almighty, the creator of the heavens and the earth, the One with all power and all authority – He hears my voice when I talk to Him! When I pray – the Living God is listening to the sound of my prayer!

I am sure we have all been in times of prayer that have felt tough. The words don't come easily, the passion doesn't seem to be there, and it seems like the heavens are brass. In those times we wonder, is anyone there? Is anyone listening? Am I just talking to myself? Are my words just hitting the ceiling?

No! We can have a confidence and an assurance today – He hears us! Always! His eyes are always on us and His ear is always attentive, listening out for the sound of our prayer.

The prophet Daniel found out this wonderful truth in Daniel 10. For three weeks Daniel prays and fasts over his people. But it seems like God doesn't answer. There is no immediate response. I wonder if Daniel was tempted to give up. I wonder if Daniel doubted that his prayers were even working. But he kept praying, kept fasting, kept crying out to God.

Finally, three weeks later, Daniel has an incredible encounter. Jesus Himself in a preincarnate appearance, comes to him. Jesus tells Daniel that He has come in response to Daniels words, and assures him that his words were heard (v12).

I believe that we can have that same assurance as Daniel did – our words are heard. The sound of your prayer is heard by God and God moves in response to that sound. This is the most amazing truth – my words move God! Heaven responds to the sound of my prayer!

Jesus actually tells Daniel that He began to move the very first day that Daniel opened his mouth to pray. How remarkable! All those days when it looked like nothing was happening, all those days when Daniel must have wondered "are my prayers working?" – heaven was listening all the time. Jesus was moving from the very first moment that Daniel began to pray!

Jesus' explanation to Daniel can be difficult for us to understand but it seems like there was a resistance in the heavenly realms from the powers of darkness, and some kind of warfare was going on, with Jesus and the archangel Michael fighting and defeating a territorial spirit that was over the kingdom of Persia. All the while Daniel was on earth praying. It seemed like Daniel, although he was unaware, was involved in this spiritual conflict between darkness and light and his prayers aided God's angelic forces in their fight against satan.

Our prayers are more powerful than we realise. The sound of our prayers are not just heard by God but they are heard by angels and by the powers of darkness. The sound of our praying moves the hand of God, releases angel armies and causes the powers of darkness to flee! The sound of your voice in prayer strengthens angels and binds the powers of the enemy. No wonder that William Cowper said, "Satan trembles when he sees the weakest saint upon their knees."

## The power of prayer

James 5:16 tells us that "The prayer of a righteous person is powerful and effective." Here are some of the stories of answered prayer in church history that have impacted my life the strongest.

### George Muller

George Muller was a remarkable man of prayer and faith who built orphanages for children in the 1800s, housing over 10,000 orphans. Muller never asked for donations but trusted totally in a God who answered prayer. One of the most well-known stories from his life is as follows:

"The children are dressed and ready for school. But there is no food for them to eat," the housemother of the orphanage informed George Mueller. George asked her to take the 300 children into the dining room and have them sit at the tables. He thanked God for the food and waited. George knew God would provide food for the children as he always did. Within minutes, a baker knocked on the door. "Mr. Mueller," he said, "last night I could not sleep. Somehow, I knew that you would need bread this morning. I got up and baked three batches for you. I will bring it in." Soon, there was another knock at the door. It was the milkman. His cart had broken down in front of the orphanage. The milk would spoil by the time the wheel was fixed. He asked George if he could use some free milk. George smiled as the milkman brought in ten large cans of milk. It was just enough for the 300 thirsty children.

© https://www.georgemuller.org/devotional/a-famous-story-about-mullers-faith

### Jim Cymbala

When Jim and Carol Cymbala went to Brooklyn Tabernacle in the early 1970s, according to Jim Cymbala, "More people were turning to Crack than to Christ." He described the dismal early days in his book Fresh Wind Fresh Fire. They had no training for ministry, no money, and only a handful of members.

Before long, seeing few victories and feeling personally defeated, the discouraged pastor decided he needed to quit. It was during that dark period he received a distinct and unexpected call from God to lead the people to pray. The next time he was before the church, he told them about his strange call from the Lord to focus on prayer.

The following Tuesday night, about a dozen members joined the pastor for prayer. They joined hands, stood in a circle and prayed. Five minutes later, they were finished. They obviously weren't sure yet how to conduct a prayer meeting, but they had taken the first steps. Over the next few years, Brooklyn Tabernacle would become known around the country and around the world as a praying church.

Pastor Jim would tell the people "From this day on the prayer meeting will be the barometer of our church. What happens on a Tuesday night will be the gauge by which we will judge success or failure. No matter what I preach or what we claim to believe in our heads, the future will depend upon our times of prayer."

Today, about 10,000 people every Sunday wait in line to attend Brooklyn Tabernacle.

Jim Cymbala traces it all to that call from the Lord so long ago to build a praying church, and to make the weekly prayer meeting the most important service of the week.

It didn't start big, but it grew. The first Tuesday night prayer meeting of a few members gathered in a circle is now 3,000 people a week crowding into the church to call upon the Lord. The prayer meeting officially begins at 7 p.m. but people start pouring in at 5 p.m. to pray for the prayer meeting!

© https://churchleaders.com/pastors/pastor-articles/309507-brooklyn-tabernacle-church-prayer-built-kie-bowman.html

Rees Howells: Dunkirk and the Battle of Britain

When the Second World War broke out the prayer meetings at Wales Bible College (led by Rees Howells) became a daily event. Every evening from 7:00 p.m. to midnight and often later, the students and staff met to pray. Every week and often for days at a time there were whole days of prayer. It seems that God would lay one or another aspect of the war on the heart of Rees Howells or one of the other prayers, and the whole community would intercede.

Did God answer those prayers?

In May 1940 as Hitler's blitzkrieg rolled across France and the Low Countries, the Bible College prayed that he would be stopped.

Norman Grubb records: "May 27, 2.45 p.m. (from Rees Howells' diary) 'It is as much as I can do to believe today. The news between the two [prayer] meetings was awful – hell upon earth.' On May 28 Mr. Howells again was alone with God. In the meetings the prayer was for God to intervene at Dunkirk and save our men; and as the Spirit came upon them in prayer and supplication, what one prayed at the end expressed the assurance given to all: 'I feel sure something has happened.'"

On May 24, 1940 Hitler had given an order to halt the armoured columns driving toward the trapped British and French troops. This order remains substantially unexplained to this day. On and after May 28th, in 'the miracle of Dunkirk,' hundreds of thousands of British and French soldiers were rescued. Did God intervene? Rees Howells and the Wales Bible College believed it was so.

Rees Howells had received assurance from the Holly Spirit that the College would be protected from enemy air attacks. Though Swansea, where the College was located, received several major raids, not one bomb fell on College property.

Norman Grubb records that on September 11, "with the Battle of Britain over London and the south of England at its fiercest, Rees Howells wrote 'There have been so many places bombed in London, even Buckingham Palace has been touched. I was burdened to pray for the King and Queen, and I believe our prayer will be answered. I am just watching how God will take hold of the enemy.'"

"September 12. 'We prayed last night that London would be defended and that the enemy would fail to break through, and God answered prayer. Unless God can get hold of this devil and bind him, no man is safe. If we have protection for our properties, why not get protection for the country?'"

"September 14. 'Because we have believed, God has made known to us what is to come to pass. Every creature is to hear the Gospel; Palestine is to be regained by the Jews; and the Saviour is to return.'"

Grubb notes that: "After the war, Air Chief Marshal Lord Dowding, Commander-in-Chief of Fighter Command in the Battle of Britain, made this significant comment: "Even during the battle one realized from day to day how much external support was coming in. At the end of the battle one had the sort of feeling that there had been some special Divine intervention to alter some sequence of events which would otherwise have occurred."

© http://www.ww2christianfiction.com/rees-howells-dunkirk-battle-britain/

## Hebridean Revival

"In a small cottage by the roadside in the village of Barvas lived two elderly women, Peggy and Christine Smith. They were eighty-four and eighty-two years old. Peggy was blind and her sister almost bent double with arthritis. Unable to attend public worship, their humble cottage became a sanctuary where they met with God. To them came the promise: "I will pour water upon him that is thirsty and floods upon the dry ground." They pleaded this day and night in prayer.
One-night Peggy had a revelation, revival was coming, and the church of her fathers would be crowded again with young people! She sent for the minister, the Rev. James Murray MacKay, and told him what God had shown her, asking him to call his elders and deacons together for special times of waiting upon God. In the same district a group of men praying in a barn experienced a foretaste of coming blessing.

One night as they waited upon God a young deacon rose and read part of the twenty-fourth Psalm: "Who shall ascend into the hill of the Lord? Or who shall stand in His holy place? He that hath clean hands and a pure heart; who hath not lifted up his soul unto vanity, nor sworn deceitfully. He shall receive the blessing from the Lord." Turning to the others he said: "Brethren, it seems to me just so much humbug to be waiting and praying as we are, if we ourselves are not rightly related to God." Then lifting his hands toward heaven, he cried: "Oh God, are my hands clean? Is my heart pure?" He got no further but fell prostrate to the floor. An awareness of God filled the barn and a stream of supernatural power was let lose in their lives. They had moved into a new sphere of God realisation, believing implicitly in the promise of revival.

In 1949, the Isle of Lewis in the Hebrides experienced a massive revival which spread throughout the entire island. It filled the church with the youth, extended through even the most resistant communities and brought thousands of lost souls to Christ. It was a truly remarkable revival."

© http://www.evanwiggs.com/revival/history/hebpray.html

## He wants to hear you!

These are just a handful of countless stories of God hearing and answering prayer. I share them as an encouragement to you that God does hear and answer prayer, and lives and even nations are changed as God moves in response to the sound of our prayers.

When Jesus' disciples asked Him to teach them to pray, He told His disciples to pray like this: "Our Father". These are the first two words of what has become known as the Lords Prayer. Our Father. Think about that for a moment. Those two words changed prayer forever. They changed the way we approach God forever. Now I no longer approach Him as a slave or a servant. I am no longer coming to a distant Deity. I am talking to my Father in Heaven. I come as a child of God. I position myself as His son.

Samuel Chadwick said:

*"Prayer is the privilege of sons, and the test of sonship. Our Lord bases prayer on personal relationship. He taught us to call God our Father, and the implication of sonship changes the whole aspect of prayer. Whatever difficulties may remain, intercourse must be possible between father and child, and to suggest that a child may not ask of a father would be to empty the terms of all meaning. It is a child's*

*right to ask, and it is a father's responsibility to hear in affectionate sympathy and discerning love. The wonder is not that God hears prayer, but that He is our Father. The greater wonder includes the less. The revelation that God is Father establishes the possibility and reasonableness of prayer. The one establishes the other. God would not be Father if His children could not pray. All the teaching of Jesus about the supremacy of the child-heart in the kingdom of God is rank blasphemy if God is not our Father. The relationship carries with it accessibility, intimacy, and fearless love. The basis of prayer is sonship. Prayer is possible and reasonable because it is filial."*

Now we see why God loves to hear our prayer. One of the greatest sounds in my life is the sound of my two young children. There is nothing greater than when I hear them say "Daddy". Sometimes it is a shout of need; they want something that I can provide. Sometimes it is a joyful sound when I walk in through the door after a trip away. Sometimes they just want me to respond so that they are assured that I am there and paying attention. But there can be no greater sound for a father than when his children call his name.

This is why God loves to hear us pray. He doesn't hear our prayers because they are sophisticated or contain amazing theology or beautiful oratory. No, He hears us because we are His children.

That is why He tells us to ask.

"Ask Me, and I will make the nations your inheritance, the ends of the earth your possession." (Psalm 2:8)

Whether we are asking for nations or for daily bread (or anything in between), God wants us to ask. Why? Because He wants to hear the sound of His children's voices.

E.M.Bounds said *"God conditions the very life and prosperity of His cause on prayer. "Ask of Me" is the condition. Upon this universal and simple promise, men and women of old laid themselves out for God. They pray and God answered their prayers and the cause of God was kept alive in the world by the flame of their praying"*

At the grave of Lazarus Jesus would make this wonderful declaration *"Father, I thank You that You have heard Me. I knew that You always hear Me"* (John 11:41-42).

Jesus knows who He is – a son. He knows who God is – His Father. Because of that Jesus has an unshakeable confidence and a deep assurance – God always hears Him. Today we can have that same confidence and same assurance. Whenever we open our mouths to pray – God hears. Not sometimes, always. Why? Not because of the greatness of our prayer, but because of who I am and who He is – I am His child and He is a good good Father.

In her beautiful song "Doves Eyes", Misty Edwards sings:

> *I believe You are listening*
> *I believe that You move at the sound of my voice*
> *I believe You are listening*
> *I believe that You move at the sound of my voice*

## When there are no words

Have you ever been in a situation when you don't know what to pray? You come before God and you open your mouth, but you just don't have the words? Sometimes the need can be so overwhelming and your situation so great than any words found in the English language just fall short.

But this is the beauty of God. His ear doesn't just hear our words.

In Psalm 5 David tell us:

*"Listen to my words, Lord, consider my sighing. Hear my cry for help, my King and my God, for to You I pray. In the morning, Lord, You hear my voice; in the morning I lay my requests before You and wait expectantly."*

When we consider prayer, we can perhaps understand David asking God to hear his voice and his requests. But David also asks God to consider his sighing! He asks God to hear his cry!

Could it be that God doesn't just hear your words, but He hears your cries too? Could he even hear your sighs? Could the sound of your sigh be considered as prayer in the ears of God?

Hebrews 5:7 gives us a little insight into Jesus' prayer life:

*"During the days of Jesus' life on earth, He offered up prayers and petitions with fervent cries and tears to the One who could save Him from death, and He was heard because of His reverent submission."*

We see on occasions such as Mark 7, when Jesus let out a deep sigh as He looked up to heaven (v34) and at Lazarus' graveside, where He prayed no audible prayer, but instead allowed His tears to flow (John 11:35)

When you cry, your tears produce a sound that God responds to. Even a sigh or a groan is the sound of prayer to God.

Samuel Chadwick said "Prayer is more than words, because it is at its mightiest when wordless"

"During that long period, the king of Egypt died. The Israelites groaned in their *slavery and cried out, and their cry for help because of their slavery went up to God. God heard their groaning and He remembered His covenant with Abraham, with Isaac and with Jacob." (Exodus 2:24-25)*

Even our groaning is a sound that goes up to heaven and a sound that heaven responds to.

Sometimes when we don't have the words to pray or we are so desperate that our words seem inadequate or we are so exhausted that our minds can't concentrate enough to formulate words….it is in those moments, when we are in God's presence and the tears flow, or a deep sigh is released or a groan comes from deep within us….we are producing sounds that count as precious prayers to God. It is the sound of His children crying out to Him, and God cannot resist those sounds.

One of the great mysteries of the Holy Spirit is how He prays through us when we don't have the words to say.

*"In the same way, the Spirit helps us in our weakness. We do not know what we ought to pray for, but the Spirit Himself intercedes for us through wordless groans."*
*(Romans 8:26)*

I find this kind of prayer the most powerful of all. This is not when I am praying with the help of the Holy Spirit, but the Holy Spirit Himself is praying through me. When the Holy Spirit prays through me like this, I often have no idea what I am praying for. All that comes out of me is groans or tears. Have you ever found yourself crying for no apparent reason in God's presence? Have you ever found yourself just groaning as you pray? This is the Holy Spirit praying through you, not using words, bypassing your mind, but nevertheless releasing a sound that the Father hears. I call it perfect prayer because it is always in line with the will of God, because your mind can't get in the way to mess it up! God is simply using your spirit as a womb as He seeks to birth something on the earth.

Paul talked about this kind of prayer being like the pains of childbirth (Galatians 4:19). This kind of prayer can be messy, noisy, confusing, even a little frightening, but it is one of the most powerful experiences we can have.

Daniel Nash (1775-1831) served as Charles Finney's personnel intercessor.
He was key to the revival that followed Finney's ministry. When God would direct where a meeting was to be held, Father Nash would slip quietly into town and seek to get two or three people to enter into a covenant of prayer with him. Sometimes he had with him a man of similar prayer ministry, Abel Clary. Together they would begin to pray fervently for God to move in the community.

One record of such is told by Leonard Ravenhill: "I met an old lady who told me a story about Charles Finney that has challenged me over the years. Finney went to Bolton to minister, but before he began, two men knocked on the door of her humble cottage, wanting lodging. The poor woman looked amazed, for she had no extra accommodations. Finally, for about twenty-five cents a week, the two men, none other than Fathers Nash and Clary, rented a dark and damp cellar for the period of the Finney meetings (at least two weeks), and there in that self-chosen cell, those prayer partners battled the forces of darkness."
Another record tells: "On one occasion when I got to town to start a revival, a lady contacted me who ran a boarding house. She said, 'Brother Finney, do you know

a Father Nash? He and two other men have been at my boarding house for the last three days, but they haven't eaten a bite of food. I opened the door and peeped in at them because I could hear them groaning, and I saw them down on their faces. They have been this way for three days, lying prostrate on the floor and groaning. I thought something awful must have happened to them. I was afraid to go in and I didn't know what to do. Would you please come see about them?' 'No, it isn't necessary,' Finney replied. 'They just have a spirit of travail in prayer.'"

How wonderful is our Father?! Not only does He hear our words, but He hears our sighs, our groans and our tears.

But He is even more wonderful than that!

In 1 Samuel 1 we read of Hannah, a barren woman who was desperate for a child. Going into the temple she prayed to God. We read that "Hannah was praying in her heart, and her lips were moving but her voice was not heard" (v13).

When it says her voice was not heard, of course it means that her voice was not heard by Eli the observant priest. But her voice was of course heard by God. Even though Hannah was making no audible sound, her silence still spoke volumes to God. The inner longing of her heart produced a sound that God heard. Psalm 37 tells us that God gives us the desires of our hearts (v4). He not only hears our words, but He hears our desires, our longings, our unspoken requests. Even our silence produces a sound that heaven hears! God would hear Hannah's unspoken prayer and answer by giving her not only a son, but a prophet!

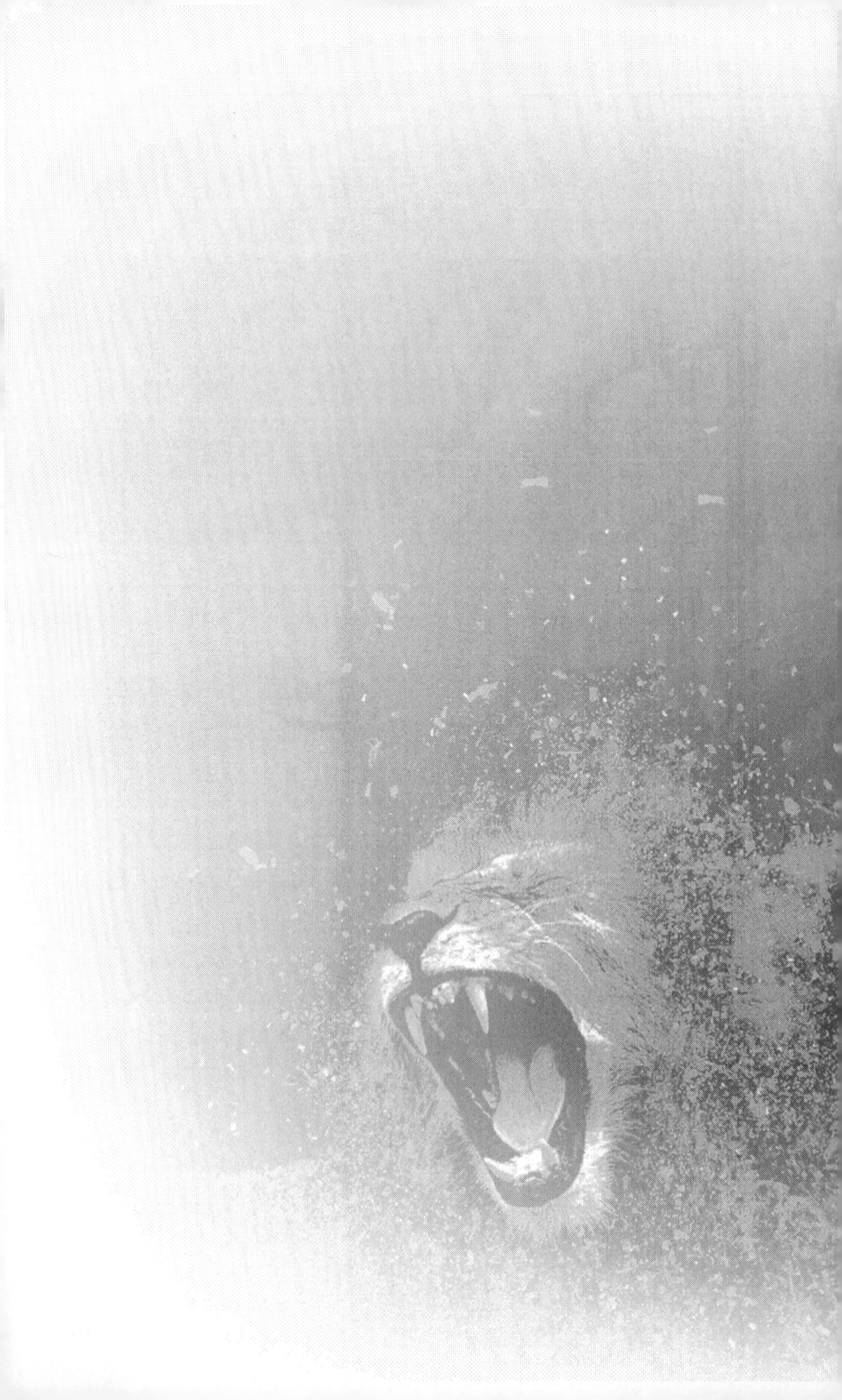

# THE SOUND OF PRAISE

*"Shout for joy to the Lord, all the earth, burst into jubilant song with music"*
*(Psalm 98:4)*

It was the first time I had ever been involved in crusade ministry. I was in Kenya, Africa, part of the ministry team of a friend of mine who was preaching the gospel to thousands of people. As I wandered around the crusade field one night, I enquired as to what the tent was that was placed at the side of the main stage. "Oh, that is the demon tent" came the response, as if it was the most obvious explanation! "Ok" came my response. "And what is a demon tent?" Being patient with me, the usher I was talking to explained that this was where people who were suffering from demonic possession were taken to receive ministry.

I had never seen this kind of ministry before and so my curiosity led me into the tent. What I encountered next will stay with me for the rest of my life.

A young girl, around 12 years old, named Lette was writhing around on the floor and making some horrendous screaming noises. Lette had been sick, and in her desperation her mother had taken her to the local witch doctor. But in attempting to cure Lette, the witch doctor had also opened a door into which the enemy had entered. Possessed by supernatural strength, a group of grown men were struggling to hold her down.

As I walked over to this scene everyone stopped and looked at me. I realised that they were expecting me to somehow sort this situation out! Little did they know that I was a complete novice at this! The only thing I could think of to do was to point at Lette and in my most authoritative voice declare, "Come out in the name of Jesus!" I stood back and waited. Had it worked?!

Imagine my shock when the demon spoke back to me through the young girl. "There are nine of us and we are not going anywhere!"

I looked to the men around me, all of us seemingly clueless and unsure as to how to proceed.

I don't know whose idea it was, but someone in that group came up with the decision to worship and praise. And so right there in that tent, this small group of Africans and one Englishman began to lift our voices and release a sound of praise and a sound of worship.

After a few moments the demon spoke again: "Could you stop singing? I don't like it!" That was when I made this life changing discovery – the sound of my praise irritates the devil! There was only one thing we could do – sing louder!

As we continued to lift up the name of Jesus and declare the greatness of God, one by one those demons left that little girl. She came up to me the next evening saying "Praise Jesus" with a big smile on her face – she had been completely delivered!

This is the power of praise! In Psalm 149 we are exhorted to make a sound of praise to God. We are commanded to sing, dance and make music.

As we create a sound of praise, there is power in that praise to bind the enemy as our praises are turned into a double-edged sword in our hands:

> Hallelujah! Praise the Lord!
> It's time to sing to God a brand-new song
> so that all His holy people will hear how wonderful He is!
>
> May Israel be enthused with joy because of Him,
> and may the sons of Zion pour out
> their joyful praises to their King.
>
> Break forth with dancing!
> Make music and sing God's praises with the rhythm of drums!
>
> For He enjoys His faithful lovers.
> He adorns the humble with His beauty
> and He loves to give them the victory.
>
> His godly lovers' triumph in the glory of God,
> and their joyful praises will rise even while others sleep.
>
> God's high and holy praises fill their mouths,
> for their shouted praises are their weapons of war!
>
> These warring weapons will bring vengeance
> on every opposing force and every resistant power—to bind kings with chains and
> rulers with iron shackles.

> *Praise-filled warriors will enforce*
> *the judgment-doom decreed against their enemies.*
> *This is the glorious honour He gives to all his godly lovers.*
> *Hallelujah! Praise the Lord! (Psalm 149 – TPT)*

In his book "The Ministry of the Psalmist" Tom Inglis says:

"Although Jesus is seated at the right hand of the Father, in some mysterious way, He joins us when we praise. In the spirit realm, there are no geographical boundaries between heaven and earth, and there is a strong possibility that when we sing, the voice of the King is heard in the spirit realm. This is a sound that makes the enemy scatter.

Praise is such a powerful weapon because the King of kings leads us in the song of victory.

There is evidence that when you sing, the Holy Spirit releases His power against the enemy coming against you. There is a flow of His power that is synergistic with the flow of your praise. There is a manifestation of God's power that seems to be released quickly when we sing. When you start to sing, the Holy Spirit starts to flow with His power against the enemy and your adverse circumstances."

## Satan and the sound of praise

In his book "The Truth About Angels", Terry Law writes:

Satan was created as the ultimate musician. When he fell, his musical ability was not taken from him, but it was corrupted.

*The information about satan's musicianship comes from Ezekiel 28:13 – "the workmanship of thy tabrets and of thy pipes was prepared in thee in the day that thou wast created."*

*Pipes were apparently built into his very body. He was a master musician. I am inclined to believe that God created him with a harmony of sound and chord in the wind instruments (pipes) that was the basic structure for melody as we know it.*

*Tabrets are what we understand to be percussion instruments. They would have given him the ability to give rhythm to the music he played. In Isaiah 14:11 there is mention of the "noise of thy viols" which are six stringed instruments. This could represent all of the stringed instruments, from violins to guitars to pianos.*

*We see in this being created by God a musician who not only is able to lead others but is also a living orchestra. Satan had been given a special, very distinctive commission from God to minister unto Him and cover His glory with music through worship and praise.*

*Music is used in advertising to make us feel a certain product will change our lives. Music is a means for communicating, influencing and controlling our spirits, minds and bodies.*
*Music is a powerful vehicle for achieving positive or negative goals.*

*When Lucifer fell from heaven, a vacancy was created. However, I believe God has a plan for replacing the "anointed cherub" who fell. I believe it is the Church who is going to bathe God in the glory of worship. The Church is going to sing "love songs" to the Father. The Church is going to make the universe ring with praise and worship of God, and the time to begin is now while we are still on earth.*

## The sound of heaven

I believe that one of the reasons satan hates the sound of praise and worship is because it reminds him of what he lost – the presence of God.

Make no mistake about it, heaven is a noisy place! Heaven is filled with the sounds of praise that are continually sung and declared to God.

Revelation 4 talks about the sounds of thunder and rumblings that take place in Heaven's throne room. It goes on to talk about the sounds of glory, honour and thanks that come from the living creatures and the 24 elders. As we move on into chapter 5, we read of the sound of those elders singing a new song, telling Jesus, the Lamb how worthy He is.

These elders are then joined by "many angels, numbering thousands upon thousands, and ten thousand times ten thousand" declaring in a "loud voice", "Worthy is the Lamb".

The elders and the angels are then joined by "every creature in heaven and on earth and on the sea, and all that is in them, singing".

Can you imagine the joyous symphony of these glorious sounds of praise and worship? This is what Heaven is filled with!

Revelation 14 is another description of the sounds of worship that take place in the presence of Jesus. This time there are the sounds of rushing waters, peals of thunder, harpists playing, and God's children singing a new song to the Lamb.

In Scripture you cannot separate the manifest presence of God and the sound of praise and worship that come from His people.

David knew this, and so he made sure that when he brought the ark of God back to Jerusalem it was accompanied by the sounds of harps, lyres, tambourines, cymbals, trumpets and *"all the Israelites celebrating with all their might before God, with songs"* (1 Chronicles 13).

The Psalmist would later describe how *"God has ascended amid shouts of joy, the Lord amidst the sounding of trumpets"* (Psalm 47:5).

Something very powerful happens when we on earth begin to release a sound of praise and worship. Firstly, we are joining in with the sound of heaven, joining with angels and living creatures. We are partnering with them in declaring who God is.

Secondly, as we release the sound of praise and worship, we are inviting the realm of heaven to invade earth. We are bringing heaven's kingdom, heaven's government to earth. We are ushering in the very presence of the King Himself.

The sound of our praises causes God to ascend. That literally means that God's presence rises like a canopy over our circumstances and environment, causing the atmosphere to change and the devil to flee. For when God arises, He causes His enemies to be scattered (Psalm 68:1).

This is why our praise and worship so irritates and terrifies the devil. He knows that when he hears that sound, his time is up! Heaven is on the move!

Psalm 22:3 in the Kings James version says that God *"inhabits the praises of His people".* Wherever there is the sound of praise and worship, that is where God lives!

If you want God to turn up, praise Him! If you want Heaven to come, praise Him! He inhabits the sound of our praise. When we create that sound, who He is is made manifest on earth.

The healer dwells among a sound of praise. The deliverer dwells among a sound of praise. The provider dwells among a sound of praise. The saviour dwells among a sound of praise.

It doesn't matter where you are or what you are going through, when you release a sound of praise, heaven comes. Your sound literally transforms not only the atmosphere, but the dominant kingdom in a place.

Interestingly the Aramaic word for "Name" when talking about the name of God, is the word "shem". This is a word that has multiple meanings, once of which is "sound". So, when you speak God's Name – whether that be Yahweh, or one of His covenant titles, or the name of Jesus – you are not just speaking a name, you are releasing a sound!

It is the sound of His Name that causes darkness to tremble! It is the sound of His Name that sets the captives free! It is the sound of His Name that heals the sick, saves the lost and causes satan to flee!

"Shem" can also mean "light" or "atmosphere" again showing us powerfully the might of His Name. When I release the sound of His Name, His light breaks forth and the very atmosphere changes.

## The sound and the shaking

In Isaiah chapter 6, the prophet has a powerful experience in which he sees or is maybe even taken into the throne room of Heaven. There he sees Jesus seated on His heavenly throne. Not surprisingly, not only does Isaiah see many glorious things, but in God's presence, he hears a sound – the sound of worship.

*"Standing above Him were the angels of flaming fire, each with six wings: with two wings they covered their faces in reverence, with two wings they covered their feet, and with two wings they flew. And one called out to another, saying:*

> *"Holy, holy, holy is the Lord God,*
> *Commander of Angel Armies!*
> *The whole earth is filled with His glory!"*

*The thunderous voice of the fiery angels caused the foundations of the thresholds to tremble as the cloud of glory filled the temple!" (v2-3 – TPT)*

In the throne room of heaven, in the presence of Jesus, Isaiah can hear the sound of worship as the angels sing "Holy, holy, holy" to the One who sits on the throne. In a similar encounter in Revelation 4, John describes how "day and night, they never stop singing" (v8).

In the presence of God there is a continuous sound of worship that goes forth. It never ends – an everlasting song of celestial praise.

Why do these angels never get bored as they continuously worship God? Why doesn't their song ever change? I believe that every time they encircle the throne, they see something new and glorious about the One seated on it. With every new revolution there is a new revelation. Every time they see Him, the majesty and splendour of Jesus hits them afresh and all they can do is release a fresh sound of praise. Although the lyrics may never change, the sound is always new and alive as they live in the always increasing and always expanding revelation of who Jesus is.

If you study angels, you will soon discover that there are different kinds and ranks of angels. There are guardian angels, messenger angels, warrior angels, archangels. As far as I can work out from my studies, the seraphim, those that are mentioned here, are the closest angelic being to the person of God. The throne room is their home, proximity is their goal and worship is their purpose. The seraphim are the custodians of the holiness of God, never leaving His presence and never ceasing to worship.

Interestingly the word "seraphim" is not really a name or a title, but more a description. It means "the burning ones" or literally "the ones who are continually on fire".

It should be no surprise to those who know their God that the burning ones, the ones who are ablaze with His fire are the ones who live in His presence, gaze upon Him and know what it is to release the sound of praise and worship.

How do we become burning ones? How do we keep our passion for Jesus ablaze? How do we live on fire for God? How do we keep always on fire with our love for Him? We choose to mirror the seraphim. We make the throne room our home. The throne room has to be the place, not that we occasionally visit but the place that we live from. His presence has to be our greatest prize, our continued goal, and the place that we long for and live from more than anywhere else.

It is in the presence of God that I learn to gaze upon Him. Whether it be through the reading of Scripture or meditating on Him, I must see Him afresh. I must have a continued fresh revelation of His greatness, His goodness, His holiness, His majesty.

Once I have seen Him, I respond to Him. How? Exactly the same way that the seraphim do – by releasing a sound of adoration. The words can be ever so simple, but the sound that they contain is enough to shake the room.

Notice how the atmosphere responded to the sound of the seraphim's song:

*"At the sound of their voices, the doorposts and thresholds shook, and the temple was filled with smoke" (v4).*

The sound of adoration was so powerful that it literally shook the throne room. The sound of angelic praise caused the very foundations of the throne room to shudder. Not only that but the temple then filled with smoke, being a description of the manifest glory of God. The glory responded to the sound. The throne room responded to the sound.

If this is the power of angelic worship, how much more the power of worship when released by the children of God, the ones created in His image and likeness, the ones redeemed by His blood, called by His Name and indwelt by His Spirit?

The lyrics of your praise may be ever so simple, they may even be repetitive, but the power is in the revelation that the praise flows from. The sound of worship that comes from a heart that is caught up in a fresh revelation of God is the most powerful sound there is.

Just saying the words "Holy" or "Worthy" or "Mighty" or "Beautiful"; just saying "Abba, Father"; just releasing the phrase "Jesus, I love You" – do you realise the power behind that? When the sound that you make comes from that place of personal revelation, not only do you become a burning one as you become ablaze with the presence of God, but you change the atmosphere around you. Heaven responds to that sound. The glory of God responds to that sound. The sound of your worship is causing a heavenly shaking to take place. The cloud of God's glory is inhabiting the sound of your adoration.

In Acts 16 we read of Paul and Silas being put into prison for preaching the gospel. We find them in a terrible situation having been stripped, beaten, severely flogged, thrown into jail, put in the inner cell (the worst part of the prison) and their feet fastened in stocks. It doesn't get much worse than that!

But what do we find Paul and Silas doing?

> "About midnight Paul and Silas were praying and singing hymns to God" (v25)

In the darkest moment, racked with pain, unable to move, these two men released a sound of praise and worship. Can you imagine what it was like, as the sound of adoration filled that prison? Satan had incapacitated them, but he could not silence their worship.

When you are in a place where all you can do is worship, you are in the best place you could possibly be – it's miracle time!

As that sound filled the prison, so did the presence and glory of God! God responded to that sound, and that prison became heaven on earth.

> "Suddenly there was such a violent earthquake that the foundations of the prison were shaken. At once all the prison doors flew open, and everybody's chains came loose" (v26).

Heaven inhabited the sound of their praise and the very foundations of the prison were shaken. Deliverance came to the captives, not only naturally but spiritually as the jailor and his entire family would go on to be baptised.

Interestingly it was not just Paul and Silas who were set free but everyone who listened to the sound of their praise too! Your praise is bigger than you. It's about more than just your breakthrough. Your praise is more powerful and more impactful than you realise.
One of the titles of Jesus is of course the Lion of the Tribe of Judah, literally the Lion of the Tribe of Praise. When we release a sound of praise, we release the roar of the lion. The sound of a lion's roar can be heard up to five miles away. The impact of our praise and worship is more powerful and more far reaching than we realise.

In the natural, lions will mostly roar at night. The thinner air means that the sound of their roar can travel further. Here is a great secret – our worship is most powerful in the dark! It is when we are in our midnight hour, when we are at our lowest point, when the pain is the greatest, the strongholds around us at their tightest, in that moment, when we release a sacrifice of praise, that sound will amplify and things begin to shake.

As God inhabits the sounds of our praise, fear begins to shake, sickness begins to shake, lies begin to shake, shame begins to shake. All around us the walls of our limitations begin to shake, the chains of restriction and bondage begin to fall off. The sound of our praise is mixed with the sounds of chains falling and the enemy crumbling.

This shaking is also found in the gospel writers' description of Jesus entering Jerusalem on the donkey.

Matthew describes how as Jesus entered Jerusalem both the "crowds that went ahead of Him and those that followed shouted, *"Hosanna to the Son of David! Blessed is He who comes in the name of the Lord! Hosanna in the highest!"* (Matthew 21:8-9)

Jesus was literally sandwiched between two crowds – one in front and one behind, both praising Him. Jesus was seated in the midst of the sound of adoration, enthroned in the praises of His people. Wherever there is the sound of praise, you will always find the presence of Jesus in the midst.

The result of the presence of Jesus and the accompanying sound of praise was that the whole city was stirred (v10). The Greek word for "stirred" here is "seio" which means "shaking". So again, we see the fruit of the sound of praise – a shaking! The footnote in the Passion Translation says, "the city was shaken like an earthquake". Here it is a city itself which is shaken, the sound of the presence of Jesus reverberating among the streets and homes.

Are we living in a day when once again entire cities will be shaken by the presence of Jesus? Are we living in a day when political systems, business empires, education, the arts, media, culture, entire belief systems will be shaken as the manifest presence of Jesus invades our cities, towns and villages?

Is it possible that there will be such a shaking that the atmosphere and culture of a city is transformed to one of joy, hope and righteousness?

Is it possible that we are living in a day when salvation doesn't just come to homes but to entire cities and regions?

The prophet Haggai spoke of a day when God would shake all nations (Haggai

2:7) whilst the writer of Hebrews spoke of a day when at the sound of His voice everything that can be shaken will be shaken, so that the one thing that can not be shaken (The Kingdom of God) would remain (Hebrews 12:26-27).

It is time for the Church to release a sound of praise like never before, to create that sound that the King can dwell in the midst of, to be that voice of change and transformation, to partner with the angels in releasing a sound that will shake cities and nations.

When a sound is made, that sound doesn't just stay at its point of origin. Instead the sound travels through waves and vibrations. Likewise, when our praise is released it travels vertically, reaching the throne room of God, and also horizontally, changing and transforming our world as heaven invades earth through the sound of our praise.

In his book "The Ministry of the Psalmist", Tom Inglis writes:

> *"That day they offered great sacrifices, an exuberant celebration because God had filled them with great joy. The women and children raised their happy voices with all the rest. Jerusalem's jubilation was heard far and wide."*
> *(Nehemiah 12:43 – The Message)*

*"The people's thankfulness was heard outside the walls of Jerusalem as an exuberant, joyful celebration. Likewise, thanksgiving is a sound that should be heard beyond the walls of the local church. When there is thanksgiving in the lives of those within the church, it won't be long before those who are unchurched will hear the sound. Our thankfulness to God for giving us eternal life magnifies the reality of who God is to others, who are yet to meet Him. Surely part of our mandate for the local church is to entice people into a joyful atmosphere of thanksgiving, for in that place they will find God's presence and His power.*

*Our thankfulness to God for His salvation and goodness will be a sound that will witness and draw the unchurched into God's house, leading them to repent."*

## **A revival of worship**

The book of Amos quoted in Acts 15 declares a day when God would restore the tent of David back to the heart of His redeemed people.

Unlike the Tabernacle of Moses there was no altar, no regular animal sacrifices, no showbread. The only thing David's Tent contained was the ark – representing God's presence. In David's tent there was 24-hour worship, a continuous sound of praise being released. This worship was accompanied by musical instruments, singing, dancing, standing, kneeling, bowing, raised hands and clapping. It was noisy, passionate, skilful and prophetic.

God links the rebuilding of David's tent with the salvation of the nations in the last days (Amos 9:11-12).

I believe that there can be little doubt that there has been a huge shift that has taken place in the worship ministry over the past few decades. Singing and music is now perhaps the most central part of our church services. Musicians on the whole have become better equipped and trained. New songs are released on an almost daily basis whilst through physical albums or internet downloads or streaming we can have access to worship music 24 hours a day.

However, there is a big concern as I travel the world and visit dozens and dozens of churches each year. Although we sing more songs than ever before, I believe the sound of true worship is becoming less and less. Out of the all churches that I visit I can say that it is the minority when I come out and think, "Wow, we really worshipped God this morning".

I believe that congregation members are no longer responding to what God is doing within them, but they are responding to what the musicians and singers are doing on the stage. Likewise, we have talented worship leaders who know how to craft a set list but don't truly know how to lead people into worship. In most services I attend we go from song to song to song but there is no space for people to actually worship. It is almost like we worship the song and not the God we are singing about! That is if the song is about God in the first place! After all, there is another growing trend, a huge proportion of songs, that are not about God but are actually about us! These can be useful as faith confessions and declarations, but they are not worship! Worship is for Him and about Him!

Are we danger of God saying of us what He said to the people of Amos' time:

*"Away with the noise of your songs! I will not listen to the music of your harps (Amos 5:23).*

God's people were evidently making a sound, but it wasn't worship, it was just a noise. I believe we have lots of noise, but the sound of worship is rare.

There are several things that we can do to change this. Pastors and preachers must preach a glorified, exalted Jesus who reigns supreme, who is overall, who is the absolute centre of everything and the only One worthy of our praise. As people get a fresh revelation of who God is, this will then produce in them a burning heart of worship.

Secondly, we must start to sing more vertical songs that are about who God is and not who we are or what He has done for us.

Thirdly, worship leaders must give time and space for people to release their sound of worship in-between songs. We must never worship the song, but instead use the song as the launchpad into true worship.

Finally, we must teach people, not just how to sing songs but how to actually worship. Paul wrote to the Ephesians telling them to speak to one another *"in psalms, hymns, and songs from the Spirit. Sing and make music from your heart to the Lord"* (Ephesians 5:19).

When a church is truly filled with the Holy Spirit, there will be a song that comes, not from the platform, but from The Spirit. This is when the Holy Spirit so bubbles up on the inside of us, that out of our hearts comes a spiritual song, a spontaneous song, a song of love and adoration that is personal to us, our own, unique, love song to Jesus! I believe that is the sound that God is truly looking for.

The infilling of the Holy Spirit is always linked with the sound of praise. The first sign that the disciples were filled with the Holy Spirit in Acts 2 was that they produced a sound, enabled by the Spirit to declare the wonders of God (v4, 11).

Again, in Acts 10, as the Holy Spirit filled those gathered in Cornelius' house, they began to praise God in a supernatural tongue (v46).

I go into more details on the power of tongues at the end of this book but for now I would say that we have to teach on tongues, expect tongues, demonstrate tongues, and make tongues a key component of our worship times.

I believe that one of the keys to a fresh move of God's glory in our corporate worship times is to make spontaneous singing, whether that be in our known language or in tongues, to be a key element of our meetings. This is when we move away from singing with the band and we move away from singing words on a screen and every individual releases their own unique love song to Jesus.

Finally we need worship leaders and singers who are not copying a pattern or format that they have seen or observed from others, but have actually been in the throne room of heaven. They have had an encounter with God and heard heaven's sound. They then know what it is to bring that sound to earth and to release it as they minister.

Above all, we need to get back to the heart of worship, as Matt Redman's classic song so wonderfully says:

> When the music fades
> All is stripped away
> And I simply come
> Longing just to bring
> Something that's of worth
> That will bless Your heart
>
> I'll bring You more than a song
> For a song in itself
> Is not what You have required
> You search much deeper within
> Through the way things appear
> You're looking into my heart
>
> I'm coming back to the heart of worship
> And it's all about You,
> It's all about You, Jesus
> I'm sorry, Lord, for the thing I've made it

When it's all about You,
It's all about you, Jesus
© Matt Redman


## **Transformed by praise**

In Genesis 29 we read of the unusual domestic situation of Jacob and his two wives Rachel and Leah. Rachel is the one that is beautiful and loved by her husband who had worked 14 years for her. Leah on the other hand was a mistake, a disappointment. She was the one that was unloved and overlooked.

Can you imagine the pain that Leah must have felt? Can you imagine the loneliness, the jealousy, the bitterness? What a terrible situation for her to be in.

What was Leah's reaction to her painful and lonely situation? It was to have a child and name him "Reuben", saying "Surely my husband will love me now" (v32).

Leah's response was like many of ours: if I can produce something then I can somehow earn my husband's affection. If I do something, then my husband will find value in me.

Many times in life we think that our value comes from what we can produce. We think that our value comes out of the house we live in, the car we drive, the money in the bank account or the job that we have.
Sometimes even in church we think that our value is because of how significant our ministry is or how prominent we are.

Tragically sometimes even with God we think that our value and acceptance comes out of what we can do – how good my behaviour is, how often I pray, how much of the Bible I have read, whether or not I have hit the mark.

When Leah realised that despite producing a son she was still unloved, what did she do? She had another son! This one she named "Simeon" meaning the "Lord hears". It seemed like, no matter what she did, no one was listening or paying her any attention.

As her frustration grew, she had yet another baby! "Now at last my husband will become attached to me". The problem with linking our value and acceptance to what we produce is that it will never be enough. There will always be a bigger house or a better job that seems just out of reach. In church there will always be someone who seems to be more significant than we are. With God, self-works are like a hungry leech that always demands more. When we think we have done everything we can, self-works demand "do more" and then God will be pleased.

The result of trying to satisfy our frustration and pain with self-works and self-efforts are that they lead to more frustration and more pain, leaving us an exhausted and burnt out mess!

But notice what happens in verse 35. Now Leah gives birth again but names her son "Judah" saying "this time I will praise the Lord".

This time her focus changes. This time there is a change of emphasis. This time she takes her pain, her frustration, her loneliness and turns it into a declaration of praise. She takes her eyes of herself and begins to release a sound of praise. For Leah it is no longer about Jacob and Rachel. She is no longer concerned whether she was being seen, or heard or loved – now her only goal was to praise God.

At that the Bible says, "Then she stopped having children" (v35).

At the sound of her praise the cycle of frustration ended, the cycle of continually having to prove herself was over. Something had changed. Something had shifted.

This is what praise has the power to do!

Only praise has the power to end negative, destructive cycles in our lives. Whether they are unhealthy habits, addictions, cycles of sin or poisonous attitudes of bitterness, shame, low self-esteem or unforgiveness; we will always be a prisoner to these things until we start to praise our way out.

The sound of our praise has the power to break chains and bring us into a place of freedom and wholeness.

This is why, when God commanded the children of Israel to march, He told them that Judah had to be first. Judah must always be first. The sound of praise must go before us. Our first response, our first reaction to all the frustrations of life must be to praise God.

There is nowhere that your praise can't be heard.

Stuck in the belly of a whale, filled with regret and pain over his disobedience, Jonah began to shout praises to God (Jonah 2:9). Even there in the darkness, in the remoteness, God heard the sound of Jonah's praise. He commanded the whale to release Jonah.

Some may feel like their disobedience has left them stuck. They feel far off course, they feel totally alone, and it seems like there is no way out. But even in that situation God is not deaf to the sound of your praise. Begin to praise Him right now. Begin to shout praises to God.

God hears and then He acts. He commands things to shift and change. He responds to the sound of your praise. Circumstances respond to the sound of His voice as He speaks and commands what is confining you to let you go.

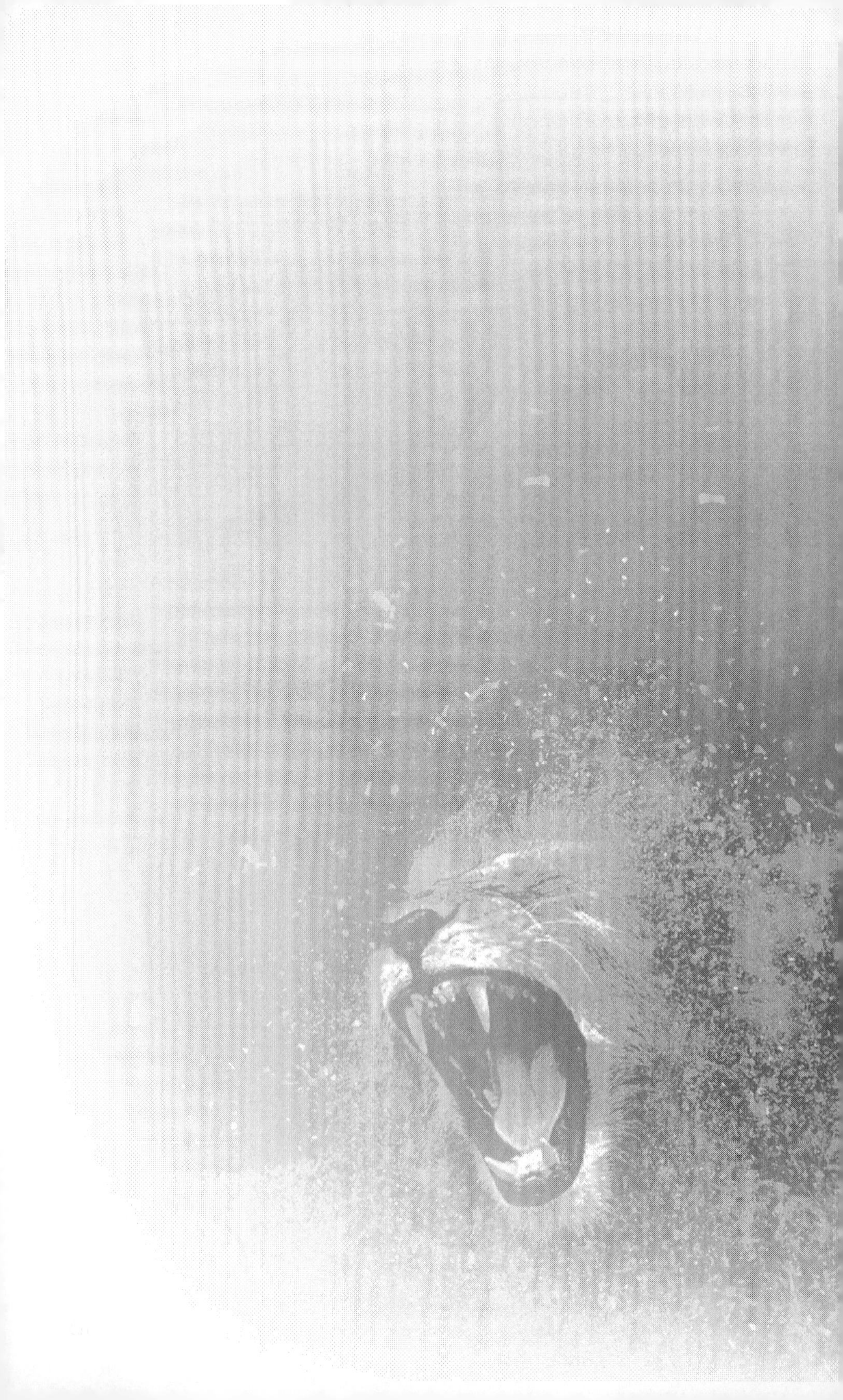

# THE ALPHA AND OMEGA OF SOUND

*"Now the earth was formless and empty, darkness was over the surface of the deep, and the Spirit of God was hovering over the waters." (Genesis 1:2)*

It all began with a sound.

Some scientists describe it as a "Big Bang"; Scripture describes it as the Voice of God. Here is a picture of a world that is without form. Totally empty. A dark void. Chaos. Nothingness. No land mass, no people, no animals. Nothing.

Just the Holy Spirit: hovering, brooding over the void.

And then into the midst of that nothingness came a sound:

*"And God said, 'Let there be light'" (v3)*

What are words? They are spoken sound. In the midst of the emptiness and the nothingness, God released His Word. He articulated a sacred sound and it was through this Word that "all things were made" (John 1:3).

The darkness responded to the sound of His Word and suddenly light appeared. The first thing God created, and it came through the sound of His voice.

As you read through the account of creation as recorded in Genesis 1 you can see the same pattern each day. Firstly, God said, "let there be" – He released the sound of His voice into the void and the Word took on shape and form and matter and became something. Then God named what He had created, the sound of His voice bringing identity and purpose.

## Creation's song

In his book "The Magicians Nephew", C.S.Lewis beautifully describes the creation of Narnia by the Christ-like figure of the lion Aslan. Lewis writes majestically of how Aslan sung creation into being:

*In the darkness something was happening at last. A voice had begun to sing. It was very far away and Digory found it hard to decide from what direction it was coming. Sometimes it seemed to come from all directions at once. Sometimes he almost thought it was coming out of the earth beneath them. Its lower notes were deep enough to be the voice of the earth herself. There were no words. There was hardly even a tune. But it was, beyond comparison, the most beautiful noise he had ever heard. It was so beautiful he could hardly bear it. The horse seemed to like it too; he gave the sort of whinny a horse would give if, after years of being a cab horse, it found itself back in the old field where it had played as a foal, and saw someone whom it remembered and loved coming across the field to bring it a lump of sugar.*

*"Gawd!" said the Cabby. "Ain't it lovely?"*

*Then two wonders happened at the same moment. One was that the Voice was* suddenly joined by other voices, more voices than you could possibly count. They were in harmony with it, but far higher up the scale: cold, tingling, silvery voices. The second wonder was that the blackness overhead, all at once, was blazing with stars. They didn't come out gently, one by one, as they do on a summer evening. One moment there had been nothing but darkness; next moment a thousand, thousand points of light leaped out: single stars, constellations, and planets, brighter and bigger than any in our world. There were no clouds. The new stars and the new voices began at exactly the same time. If you had seen and heard it, as Digory did, you would have felt quite certain that it was the stars themselves who were singing, and that it was the first Voice, the deep one, which had made them appear and made them sing.

"Glory be!" said the Cabby. "I'd ha' been a better man all my life if I'd known there were things like this."

The voice on the earth was now louder and more triumphant; but the voices in the sky, after singing loudly with it for a time, began to get fainter. And now something else was happening.

Far away, and down near the horizon, and the sky began to turn grey. A light wind, very fresh, began to stir. The sky, in that one place, grew slowly and steadily paler. You could see shapes of hills standing against it. All the time the voice went on singing.

The eastern sky changed from white to pink and from pink to gold. The voice rose and rose, till all the air was shaking with it. And just as it swelled to the mightiest and most glorious sound it had yet produced, the sun arose.

Digory had never seen such a sun. You could imagine that it laughed for joy as it came up. And as its beams shot across the land the travellers could see for the first time what sort of place they were in. It was a valley through which a broad, swift river wound its way, flowing eastward towards the sun. Southward there were mountains, northward there were lower hills. But it was a valley of mere earth, rock and water; there was not a tree, not a bush, not a blade of grass to be seen. The earth was of many colours; they were fresh; hot and vivid. They made you feel excited; until you saw the Singer himself, and then you forgot everything else.

It was a Lion. Huge, shaggy, and bright, it stood facing the risen sun. Its mouth was wide open in song and it was about three hundred yards away.

The Bible also describes the song that accompanied creation. The book of Job tells us that, when God created the universe, the morning stars sang together, and the angels shouted for joy! (Job 36:7)

It was the sound of heaven, the sound of His voice, the sacred song of the Father that brought everything into being. The universe responded to that sound and still responds to that sound. That sound still resonates throughout the universe as everything that was created by His sound, echoes back to Him a sound of praise.

In his book "The Ministry of the Psalmist", Tom Inglis writes:

*In God's creation there is potential for praise even at an atomic level. Jesus said that if humanity would not praise Him, the rocks would literally complain of the injustice of being denied the opportunity.*

*"But He said, "If they kept quiet, the stones would do it for them, shouting praise." (Luke 19:40 – The Message)*

*It is not surprising that the entire universe responds to the Creator with praise! Structured into the atoms making up the molecules in the rocks is the inherent capacity to praise. The inanimate objects have within them, a consciousness of the Creator and an inherent ability to respond to Him with praise. Scientists have recorded sounds coming from distant galaxies that are explained as the sound of chemical reactions. Further, it is from within the sub-atom particles where there is the sound of praise. The Bible says that the stars praise Him, the heavens sing, along with all creation.*

"Praise Him, sun and moon; praise Him, all you shining stars." (Psalm 148:3)

"The grazing meadows are covered with flocks, and the fertile valleys are clothed with grain, each one dancing and shouting for joy, creation's celebration! And they're all singing their songs of praise to You!" (Psalm 65:13 – TPT)

"Sing for joy, you heavens, for the Lord has done this; shout aloud, you earth beneath. Burst into song, you mountains, you forests and all your trees, for the Lord has redeemed Jacob, He displays His glory in Israel." (Isaiah 44:23)

"Shout for joy, O heavens, and rejoice, O earth, And break forth into singing, O mountains! For the Lord has comforted His people And will have compassion on His afflicted." (Isaiah 49:13 – Amp)

"You will go out in joy and be led forth in peace; the mountains and hills will burst into song before You, and all the trees of the field will clap their hands." (Isaiah 55:12)

"Then the trees of the forest will sing for joy before the Lord; For He comes to judge and govern the earth." (1 Chronicles 16:33 – Amp)

"Burst into songs of joy together, you ruins of Jerusalem, for the Lord has comforted His people, He has redeemed Jerusalem" (Isaiah 52:9)

"Let the ocean's waves join in the chorus with their roaring praise until everyone everywhere shouts out in unison, "Glory to the Lord!" (Psalm 98:7 – TPT)

"Beside them the birds of the heavens have their nests; They lift up their voices and sing among the branches." (Psalm 104:12 – Amp)

Because God created everything that exists, everything that exists responds to Him with praise. The universe is an endless testimony of praise to the glory of God.

"The heavens declare the glory of God; And the firmament shows His handiwork. Day unto day utters speech, And night unto night reveals knowledge. There is no speech nor language where their voice is not heard. Their line has gone out through all the earth, and their words to the end of the world. In them He has set a tabernacle for the sun" (Psalm 19:1-4)

If all of creation praises God, how much more should we, who are the pinnacle of all His creation, made in His own image and likeness?

This concept is put so brilliantly in the Hillsong United song 'So Will I':

God of creation
There at the start
Before the beginning of time
With no point of reference
You spoke to the dark
And fleshed out the wonder of light

And as You speak
A hundred billion galaxies are born
In the vapor of Your breath the planets form
If the stars were made to worship so will I
I can see Your heart in everything You've made
Every burning star a signal fire of grace
If creation sings Your praises so will I
So will I

God of Your promise
You don't speak in vain
No syllable empty or void
For once You have spoken
All nature and science follow the sound of Your voice

And as You speak
A hundred billion creatures catch Your breath
Evolving in pursuit of what You said
If it all reveals Your nature so will I
I can see Your heart in everything You say
Every painted sky a canvas of Your grace
If creation still obeys You so will I
So will I

If the stars were made to worship so will I
If the mountains bow in reverence so will I
If the oceans roar Your greatness so will I
For if everything exists to lift You high so will I

If the wind goes where You send it so will I
If the rocks cry out in silence so will I
If the sum of all our praises still falls shy
Then we'll sing again a hundred billion times

© Songwriters: Joel Houston, Benjamin Hastings, Michael Fatkin
So Will I (100 Billion X) lyrics © CAPITOL CHRISTIAN MUSIC GROUP

The Bible shows us a world that not only was brought into existence by sound but is sustained by sound.

Hebrews 1:3 tells us that everything is sustained by His powerful word. If God was ever silent, if for just one moment He stopped speaking, then all of creation would suddenly cease to exist. But He will never stops speaking, creations song will go and on and on. For even when this present earth and heaven have passed away the sound of Jesus speaking never ends (Luke 21:33).

## Releasing heavens song

As we read and study the account of creation, we also see a powerful principle that is relevant to all of our lives today.

As we read of a world that was empty, formless and dark we can see a pattern of our own lives from time to time.

Many times, it feels like our own "world" is in darkness: the darkness of pain, of suffering, of overwhelming circumstances. Many times, our lives feel void of hope, of joy or of peace. Many times, our lives feel empty of God's power, God's life, God's provision, God's presence.

What do we do when faced with our own Genesis 1 scenario?

Is it possible that as God brought light from darkness, beauty from chaos and substance from emptiness purely by the sound of His voice that we, created in His image and likeness, and filled with the same creative Spirit could do the same?

Could it be that as we sing and speak and declare God's life, God's hope, God's power, God's truth, God's promises over the barren wastelands of our lives that sickness has to respond to the sound of our voice, that lack has to respond to the sound of our voice, that darkness has to respond to the sound of our voice?

## The Barren Woman

Isaiah 54 tells us the story of a barren woman. This is a woman whose womb is dead and unable to produce life. Not only that but she doesn't even have a husband either. The chances of her having a child are zero. Not only does she have no man to help her conceive but even if she did, her body wouldn't allow her to conceive anyway.

What is God's instruction to this barren woman?

> "Sing, barren woman, you who never bore a child; burst into song, shout for joy, you who were never in labour; because more are the children of the desolate woman than of her who has a husband,' says the Lord." (Isaiah 54:1).

The Message Translation says:

*"Sing, barren woman, who has never had a baby. Fill the air with song, you who've never experienced childbirth! You're ending up with far more children than all those childbearing women."*

God tells the barren woman to sing over her barrenness, to sing over her dead womb. He tells her to create a sound over her emptiness. Sing a song of creation, sing a song of life, sing a song of hope.

I have found that the greatest thing I can do over the barren areas of my life is to declare the sound of heaven over them.

Whatever it is that may be barren in my life – finances, relationships, health, my own soul – I begin to release the sound of heaven over those areas. I sing, I speak, I declare – I release the promises of God, I release prophetic words, I declare scripture, I sing His praises, I confess who God is, I speak the Name of Jesus.

As I do this in faith, I find that my circumstances have to respond to the sound of my voice because the life of the Creator is contained within my sound. The same Word that brought creation into being is joining in with my words and, as I sing those words, together we are singing a duet that has to produce life. The same Holy Spirit that took the words of the Father and brought life out of nothingness, now takes my words and causes the same process of creation to take place over whatever it is that I am speaking over.

*"As the rain and the snow come down from heaven, and do not return to it without watering the earth and making it bud and flourish, so that it yields seed for the sower and bread for the eater, so is My word that goes out from My mouth: it will*

*not return to Me empty, but will accomplish what I desire and achieve the purpose for which I sent it." (Isaiah 55:10-11)*

David

In Psalm 57, David is on the run from King Saul. Fleeing for his life he finds himself taking refuge in a cave. Alone. Lost. Fearful. In the darkness. How will this man of God respond?

*"My heart, O God, is steadfast, my heart is steadfast; I will sing and make music. Awake, my soul! Awake, harp and lyre! I will awaken the dawn." (Psalm 57:7-8)*

David does not sit idly by, waiting for the darkness to go of its own accord. He doesn't do nothing, just hoping that one day his circumstances will change. No, instead David says, "I will awaken the dawn" – I will cause light to penetrate the darkness, I will create a new day, I will bring a new season into being!

How? He sings into the darkness. He makes music in the cave. He prophecies an awakening. He sings into being a new morning.

Job describes God as One who gives songs in the night (Job 35:10), whilst the Psalmist spoke of those who ministered to God by singing praises in the night-time (Psalm 134:1).

When we sing into the darkness, sing during the midnight hour, sing when all is lost and we can not see our way out, our sound is creating what we are declaring!

Trapped in the restrictions of the cave, David in the Spirit began to see himself singing and prophesying over nations!

*"I will praise You, Lord, among the nations; I will sing of You among the peoples"
(Psalm 57:9)*

It seems almost laughable, a man trapped in a cave, hemmed in by his enemies, singing God-songs over nations. But David's song was bigger than his environment. The sound of his song reached far beyond his own limitations.

As David awakened the dawn by singing and declaring God's praises, Psalm 108 gives us the follow up to what happened next:

> *"God has spoken from his sanctuary: 'In triumph I will parcel out Shechem and measure off the Valley of Sukkoth. Gilead is Mine, Manasseh is Mine; Ephraim is My helmet, Judah is My sceptre. Moab is My washbasin; on Edom I toss My sandal; over Philistia I shout in triumph." (Psalm 108:7-9)*

As David sung into the darkness, He heard a sound coming back to him in the echoes of the cave: "God has spoken". Truly there can be no greater word than that! As David sung into the hopelessness, God responded to the sound of David's song and spoke back to Him words of assurance, words of authority and words of victory!

No wonder David could confidently declare:

*"With God we shall gain the victory, and He will trample down our enemies." (v13)*

## John the Baptist

Scholars estimate that there were around 400 years between the last prophet of the Old Testament, Malachi, and the first of the new, John the Baptist. John would act as a bridge, closing one era and ushering in a new one.

Those 400 years are known as "The silent years" – 400 years with no new prophetic word coming to Israel.

The only spirituality God's covenant people knew was the dead religion of the Pharisees, Sadducees and teachers of the law.

It was in the midst of this that John the Baptist appears.

John is described initially, not as a preacher or a prophet or as a minister but as "a voice":

> "A voice of one calling in the desert" (Luke 3:4).

Into the 400 years of silence a new sound was heard. John was that voice in the desert, that sound in the wilderness. The barrenness and wilderness that surrounded him was a parallel to Israel's spiritual condition.

And yet into this desert the sound of John's voice rang out. It was a voice of truth, a voice of conviction, a challenging voice, a prophetic voice, an uncompromising voice, a Jesus-pointing voice.

As John spoke into the wilderness, the sound of this voice caused valleys to be filled in, mountains and hills were made low, crooked roads became straight, rough ways were made smooth. Mankind once again began to see God's salvation as the voice prepared the way for the manifestation of the Messiah (Luke 3:4-6).

This is the power of the sound of our voice when we are fully yielded to God. We have the opportunity every day to speak into the silence, to speak into the void. We become that voice over the wilderness of our lives or the barrenness of a nation. We become that prophetic voice. We speak and declare over the wasteland; we sing into the silence; we proclaim truth over the crooked places and the rough areas; we command mountains to move and every obstacle to be made low.

Our voice ushers in His Kingdom, His presence, His power and the salvation of Jesus Himself.

## **The King is Coming**

Not only did this world begin with the sound of heaven, but this age will also end with a sound from heaven too.

*"Listen, I tell you a mystery: we will not all sleep, but we will all be changed – in a flash, in the twinkling of an eye, at the last trumpet. For the trumpet will sound, the dead will be raised imperishable, and we will be changed. For the perishable must clothe itself with the imperishable, and the mortal with immortality." (1 Corinthians 15:51-53)*

*"For the Lord Himself will come down from heaven, with a loud command, with the voice of the archangel and with the trumpet call of God, and the dead in Christ will rise first." (1 Thessalonians 4:16)*

*When Jesus came to earth the first time 2000 years ago His coming was announced by the sound of angels singing:*

*"At once the angel was joined by a huge angelic choir singing God's praises: Glory to God in the heavenly heights, Peace to all men and women on earth who please him." (Luke 2:13-14 – The Message)*

The coming of Jesus is always accompanied by a sound. His second coming will be no different. This time it will be the sound of a trumpet – the last trumpet – the last sound of this age that will usher in the coming Kingdom and the return of the King.

*"Very truly I tell you, a time is coming and has now come when the dead will hear the voice of the Son of God and those who hear will live." (John 5:25)*

Think how awesome that sound will be? Here the words at Lazarus' graveside become a prophetic foreshadowing. One day instead of saying, "Lazarus come forth" He will speak the name of every person that has ever lived and command them to come forth!

Every person that has ever lived will hear the sound of His Voice and will have to respond to that sound. The earth and sea will give up its dead. The graves will be opened. Every man and woman who has ever lived will respond to the sound of His voice and stand before their Maker.

There will be no hiding place. There will be no excuses. Atheism will cease to exist in that moment. All other false gods and religions and philosophies will bow. Only one voice will matter. The One who spoke the first Word will now have the final Word. In that moment only the words that come from the mouth of Jesus will matter.

It will be a final day of judgement and justice. To those who have rejected Him they will hear the words:

*"Depart from Me, you who are cursed, into the eternal fire prepared for the devil and his angels." (Matthew 25:41)*

But to those that love Him, to those that have trusted Him, to those redeemed by His blood, to those who have thrown themselves on His grace, oh, what joy to hear the sound of His voice:

*"Well done, good and faithful servant!" (Matthew 25:23)*

*"Come, you who are blessed by My Father; take your inheritance, the Kingdom prepared for you since the creation of the world." (Matthew 25:34)*

For those, never again will they hear the sound of weeping and mourning. They will be swallowed up by the sounds of praise, adoration and rejoicing in His presence. A song of praise that will never end.

Are you listening out for the sound of that trumpet? Is your ear open, listening for the sound that announces the return of the King?

As we live in a world full of pain, injustice and hatred, deep within the hearts of the lover of God there is a sound of longing that is echoed in the heart of the Holy Spirit Himself:

*"The Spirit and the bride say "Come!" (Revelation 22:17)*

And if she listen's carefully enough, the Bride of Christ can hear a sound from heaven responding to her cry:

*"Yes, I am coming soon" (v20)*

*"Amen. Come, Lord Jesus"*

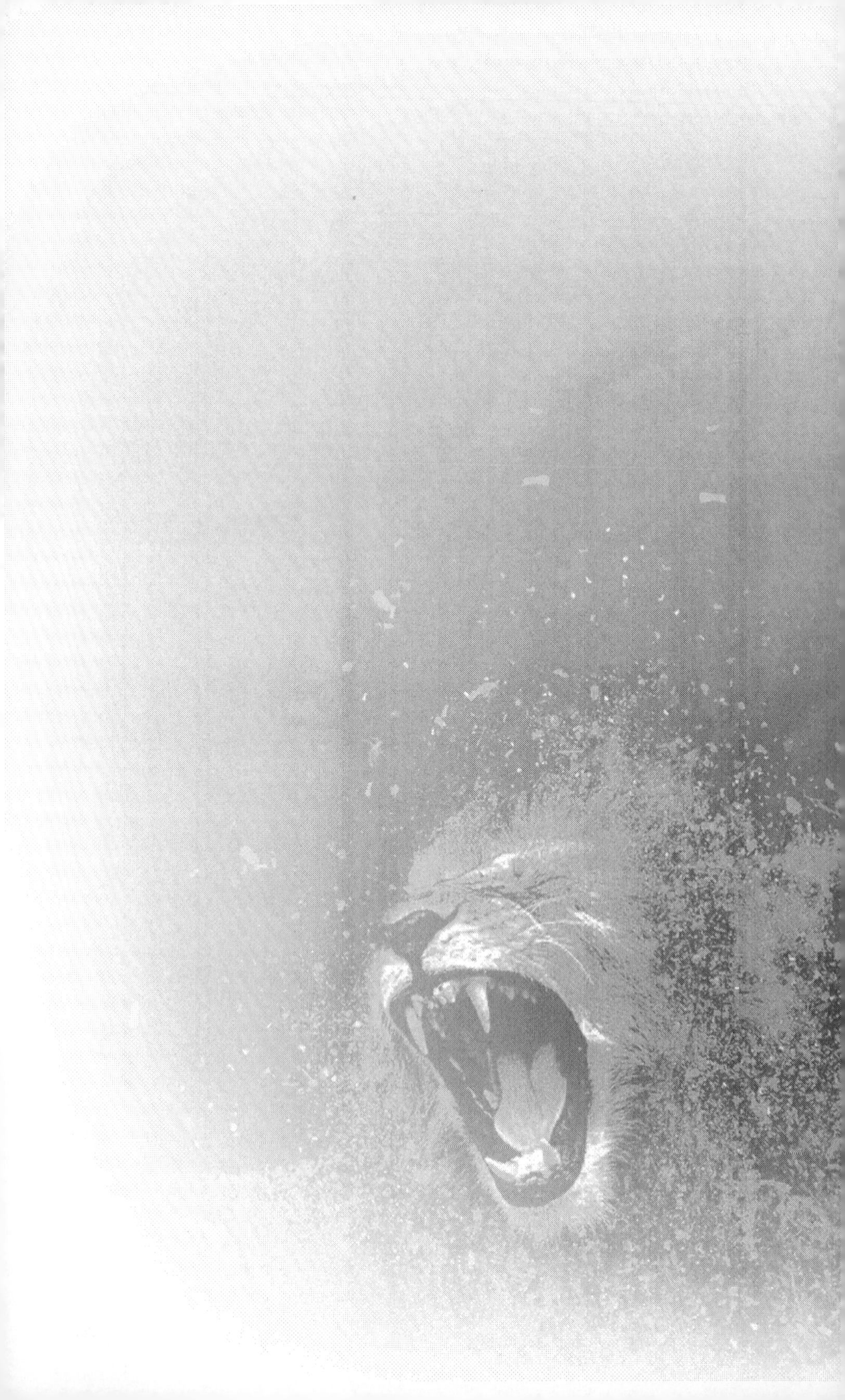

# THE SOUND OF THE LION AND THE TRUMPET

*"Has any other people heard the voice of God speaking out of fire, as you have, and lived?" (Deuteronomy 4:33)*

Myself and my brother Matthew were brought up by God-fearing parents in a Christian family. We both attended a Christian school and gave our lives to Jesus at a young age. As we grew into our teenage years though our lives seemed to go in two different paths.

As someone who took their faith very seriously, I went on a path that would lead me straight into full-time church ministry as soon as I left school. Matthew, on the other hand, had never seemed to have too deep a relationship with God and, as the years went by, he went away from God and church totally, living a sinful, rebellious lifestyle whilst pursuing a career in journalism.

My life came to a place where I was very settled and content. I loved church and was in the privileged position of being paid to spend every day there. My days were spent either in Bible study or prayer. My evenings were spent in prayer meetings or youth services. Sundays I was busy teaching God's people. The church seemed to be responding well to my ministry and I enjoyed giving myself exclusively to the family of God. Happy days. The idea of getting out of my church comfort zone, sharing the gospel with non-believers, going on an overseas mission – all of that made me shudder. I'm not an evangelist I would say, I'm not a missionary. I'm happy here just working among Christians.

One weekend something remarkable happened. My brother, who had become so hard to the things of God, attended a local "revival" that was happening in the church my parents attended. In the space of a few weeks, Matthew had got radically saved, filled with the Holy Spirit and joined an evangelistic ministry that was travelling around the country holding special services where people were getting saved and healed.

Matthew now devoted his entire life to mission and evangelism. Every spare minute he was driving around the country taking part in these evangelistic services. Then came the overseas missions – Kenya, Sierra Leone, India.

After years of Matthew mocking my Christian faith, now I was the one to think that he had gone crazy! Yes, all Christians should be sharing the gospel and going on mission, but Matthew had become a radical! He was taking things to an extreme. My safe and secure Christianity was very different to his fiery passion to reach people with the gospel no matter what the cost.

I remember the day when he quit his job to go on a mission trip to Kenya. Not just to go on vacation. I mean to literally walk out of a promising career: "I'm leaving and not coming back. I have to take the gospel to Africa".

He has gone too far this time I thought! Why can't he just settle for a nice, safe, comfortable ministry like I have? After all I'm serving Jesus too. Why does he have to go to such an extreme?

I began to justify myself: "He has a different calling to me"; "He's young, it will soon wear off and he'll settle down".

Then in January 2012 something life changing happened. I had gone away for a few days to seek God. I had no agenda; I just wanted an encounter with His presence. On the final night of this retreat, the glory of God came into the room. I fell facedown and the fire of God fell on my life. From the top of my head to the soles of my feet, it was like waves of fire were flowing through me. I felt a burning sensation in my innermost being as God fulfilled His promise to baptise in the Holy Spirit and in fire (Matthew 3:11).

After a few hours the heavy glory lifted and I stood to my feet. But from that moment on I have never been the same.

You see the Bible tells us that God's voice is heard in the fire (Deuteronomy 4:33). It was as the fire of God fell on me that I heard the sound of God. This sound was like a pulsating drum beat that was pounding away in my innermost being. The rhythm that it was playing was the sound of the lost, desperate to hear the gospel and the sound of the nations crying out for Jesus.

Suddenly all I could think about was that people needed Jesus. Now all I could think about was the nations. It was like a sound, a drum in my chest and I couldn't escape it. Heaven's sound was in me and wouldn't leave me alone.

Now I couldn't go to a soccer game without looking around me at thousands of people that didn't know Jesus and being overwhelmed. Now my every prayer seemed to be "God, give me the nations."

The sound of heaven that I constantly heard was similar to the sound that Isaiah heard when he was in the throne room of God.

> "Then I heard the voice of the Lord saying, 'Whom shall I send? And who will go for us?' And I said, 'Here am I. Send me!' (Isaiah 6:8)

It was the same sound that the Apostle Paul heard one night that caused him to alter his plans and take the gospel to the nation of Macedonia.

"During the night Paul had a vision of a man of Macedonia standing and begging him, 'Come over to Macedonia and help us.' After Paul had seen the vision, we got ready at once to leave for Macedonia, concluding that God had called us to preach the gospel to them." (Acts 16:9-10)

When you experience the fire of God, you will hear a sound within that fire – it is the sound of the nations calling you, it is the sound of the lost crying for a saviour, it is the sound of the hurting and needy desperate for His presence.

For several years I didn't do anything with that sound. I carried on with my ministry within the local church, teaching and preaching. But I was no longer content and comfortable like I had been before. The sound of the nations crying out just wouldn't leave me alone. In fact, as the years went by the sound only intensified.

Around 6/7 years after my encounter with God I was in a meeting where a man called Cleddie Keith was preaching. The title of his message was "I will not eat my bread alone!" He was challenging us: "If you have an anointing, a ministry, a word, a passion, it is not for you to keep it to yourself – it is to share with others. Take a leap of faith and follow your God-given passion and see where it will take you".

That message from Pastor Cleddie was like a trumpet blast; it was a prophetic call to action. I knew I had to respond to heaven's sound. Over the following months I began to hand over my pastoral duties in the church and finally, 8 years to the day since I encountered heaven's fire, I was released to travel the nations as a missionary evangelist.

Since that time, I have preached in many countries, seen many salvations and healings and thousands touched by the presence of God. It has meant living by faith and has at times been a huge challenge, but not one I have ever come to regret. And as I write these words, I can still hear the sound of heaven pounding in my heart – the nations, crying out for the gospel.

## The sound of trumpets

For me, when I heard the sound of heaven, it was a call to missions, to take the gospel to the nations. Your call is maybe different to my call, but one thing is for sure: the sound of heaven will always produce movement in your life.

In Numbers 10, the Bible tells us about two silver trumpets that were used to get the attention of the children of Israel in their wilderness wanderings.

> *"The Lord said to Moses: 'Make two trumpets of hammered silver, and use them for calling the community together and for the camps to set out. When both are sounded, the whole community is to assemble before you at the entrance to the tent of meeting. If only one is sounded, the leaders – the heads of the clans of Israel – are to assemble before you. When a trumpet blast is sounded, the tribes camping on the east are to set out. At the sounding of a second blast, the camps on the south are to set out. The blast will be the signal for setting out. To gather the assembly, blow the trumpets, but not with the signal for setting out.*

*'The sons of Aaron, the priests, are to blow the trumpets. This is to be a lasting ordinance for you and the generations to come. When you go into battle in your own land against an enemy who is oppressing you, sound a blast on the trumpets. Then you will be remembered by the Lord your God and rescued from your enemies. Also at your times of rejoicing – your appointed festivals and New Moon feasts – you are to sound the trumpets over your burnt offerings and fellowship offerings, and they will be a memorial for you before your God. I am the Lord your God." (Numbers 10:1-10)*

God's people were to be moved by a sound – in this case the sound of trumpets. Whether it was to assemble together for a meeting, go to battle against their enemies, begin a time of feasting or break up camp and march out to the next place, the sound of the trumpets meant "It's time to move".

It didn't matter what they were doing, they had to respond when they heard the trumpets. If they were asleep, they had to wake up. If they were at work, they had to stop. If they were eating a meal, they had to put it away. When they heard the sound of the trumpets, they had to move – they had to respond or else they would miss what God was trying to move them into.

This idea of being moved by the sound of the trumpet was one that the prophet Jeremiah would draw on. Jeremiah had been in the presence of the Lord and God had shown him that disaster was coming on the nation. Judgement was about to be poured out because of Israel's sin.

This was Jeremiah's response:
*"Oh, my anguish, my anguish! I writhe in pain. Oh, the agony of my heart! My heart pounds within me, I cannot keep silent. For I have heard the sound of the trumpet; I have heard the battle cry." (Jeremiah 4:19)*

In the presence of God, Jeremiah felt like he was hearing a trumpet blasting away on the inside of him and he had to respond. In Jeremiah's case the call to battle was a call to begin to prophesy, to begin to warn people of what was coming, to plead for people to repent. It was a call to pray and intercede for the nation, to start to declare the word of God. It was a sound, like a trumpet blast, deep within him, that he could not escape from.

When God's word comes to us, of course it brings life, peace, strength and joy. But this is only one half of the whole.

Many times heaven's sound is a call to action! It is a like a burning fire, like a pounding drum, like a trumpet being blasted on the inside of you. Something is being birthed within you – your heart is burning with a God call, a God dream, a God given passion. It is all consuming. You can not turn it on or off. The sound is heard 24/7 until you have to respond!

For my brother and myself it was the sound of the nations crying out for the gospel. For Jeremiah it was the sound of coming judgement that shook him into action. What is the sound that you can hear within you? Is it the sound of the lost? Is it the sound of injustice? Is it the sound of people needing solutions and help in a particular area of society?

What is the sound that drives you to your knees in prayer? What is the sound that you hear that keeps you awake at night? What is the people group that you hear crying out for help when you are in the presence of God? What is the sound that you have to respond to?

There came a moment when Jeremiah tried to stop his prophetic ministry because of the persecution he was getting, but when he tried he said:

*"But if I say, 'I will not mention His word or speak any more in his Name,' His word is in my heart like a fire, a fire shut up in my bones. I am weary of holding it in; indeed, I cannot." (Jeremiah 20:9)*

He could not escape the call that was within him. The sound of heaven was like a fire that just wouldn't leave him alone. He had to respond.

## The sound of the lion

In the book of Amos, the sound of heaven is described as a roaring lion:

*"Surely the Sovereign Lord does nothing without revealing His plan to His servants the prophets.*

*The lion has roared – who will not fear? The Sovereign Lord has spoken – who can but prophesy?" (Amos 3:7-8)*

When God speaks, His voice is regal and majestic. It is a sound of authority. There is glory mixed with fear – just like the roar of a lion.

Amos says that when someone hears the sound of the lion, they have to respond. For some it is the response of fear, for others it is the call to prophesy. But there is always a response. When a lion roars in the wild there is always a response. That sound produces fear in other creatures. For the other lions, they know that roar is a call – a call to start the hunt or a warning sound that danger is on the way.

But you can't ignore or dismiss the sound of the lion's roar.

Amos is saying the same thing about the sound of heaven. When you hear heaven's sound you have to respond. In the context, Amos is speaking specifically about prophecy. Amos is saying that when a prophet heard God speak, they had to prophesy, they had to release what God has told them. They can't hold it in or supress it. They have to speak.

This is what a prophetic voice is – it is someone who has been in the presence of the Lord and they have heard the lion's roar. Now that roar is in them. They have to open their mouths and release what God is saying.

Another prophet who heard the sound of heaven was the prophet Ezekiel. In Ezekiel 33, God describes his servant as a watchman.

*The word of the Lord came to me: "Son of man, speak to your people and say to them: "When I bring the sword against a land, and the people of the land choose one of their men and make him their watchman, and he sees the sword coming against the land and blows the trumpet to warn the people, then if anyone hears the trumpet but does not heed the warning and the sword comes and takes their life, their blood will be on their own head. Since they heard the sound of the trumpet but did not heed the warning, their blood will be on their own head. If they had heeded the warning, they would have saved themselves. But if the watchman sees the sword coming and does not blow the trumpet to warn the people and the sword comes and takes someone's life, that person's life will be taken because of their sin, but I will hold the watchman accountable for their blood." 'Son of man, I have made you a watchman for the people of Israel; so hear the word I speak and give them warning from me.  When I say to the wicked, "You wicked person, you will surely die," and you do not speak out to dissuade them from their ways, that wicked person will die for their sin, and I will hold you accountable for their blood.  But if you do warn the wicked person to turn from their ways and they do not do so, they will die for their sin, though you yourself will be saved." (v1-9)*

God's prophets in the Old Testament were like watchmen on the walls. They had been in the presence of God and heard the sound of heaven announcing that judgement was coming unless the people repented. Now the prophets sounded the alarm, released what God was saying and urged people to respond.

If the prophets heard the sound of heaven but didn't release that sound, then God would hold them responsible for what would happen. But if the prophets released what God was saying, now the responsibility was on the listeners: if they failed to respond to the sound of heaven, then they would be the ones responsible, not the prophets.

Jesus gave the same warning several times in the gospels: Whoever has ears to hear, let them hear.

In other words, if you hear the sound of heaven, you have to respond. If you are a prophet, you have to obey God and release what God is saying. If you hear a prophet, you can't dismiss or despise the prophetic word, you have to listen to what God is saying and respond accordingly.

## **The sound of obedience**

Whilst the prophetic voice of the Old Testament was primarily concerned with repentance and judgement, the primary purpose of the prophetic voice in the Church Age is to build up, to strengthen and to empower.

However, that does not mean the prophetic voice of the New Testament carries any less weight than the voice of the Old Covenant prophets. Whilst of course we always judge every prophetic word soberly in light of scripture, and we never replace the need for scripture with a desire for the prophetic, nevertheless, even in the Church Age, every prophetic word demands a response.

Paul put it like this in 1 Corinthians 14:8

*"Again, if the trumpet does not sound a clear call, who will get ready for battle?"*

Paul is speaking about the gift of prophesy. He makes two points, one to the prophetic voice and the other to the one receiving the prophetic word.

To the one releasing the prophetic word he is saying, the prophetic word must be a "clear call". Other translations say that the prophetic word must be certain and distinct.

Sometimes I hear prophetic words and I have no idea what the person is trying to say. It is true that prophetic words are concerning spiritual things that our human minds can not comprehend. It is also true that prophetic words can sometimes contain metaphors, symbols and images. But Paul is plain – the prophetic word must be a clear call.

Sometimes people fill a prophetic word with so much symbolism and metaphor that people have no idea what God is trying to say. Sometimes God can be trying to speak but the vessel he is using is so weird that no one is listening! Sometimes we add to what God is saying and confuse matters. Sometimes God can be speaking but mixed in are our own additions. Sometimes there can be mix of prophecy combined with false doctrine and something that is more like a Christian horoscope.

Paul says that if the trumpet call is not clear, what good is it? Some prophetic ministries do more harm than good. They use all kinds of seemingly impressive mystical language but when they have finished it is not clear – what is God actually saying?

For the prophetic people in the body of Christ, it is not enough to just hear the sound of heaven. We must learn how to communicate that sound so that it is clear what God is saying and it is applicable to people's lives.

That brings us to the second application of Paul's words. When the prophetic voice speaks it must be clear but when the person listening hears what God is saying, they must respond. The prophetic word calls them to battle, it springs them into action. Sometimes God specifically tells us to do something, sometimes he is telling us we need to repent or change an area of behaviour or thinking, but there is always a response.

When God speaks words of promise and destiny it is not fortune telling, it is not dependent on fate – it is dependent on our obedience.

Let me be clear, the prophetic only speaks to potential. The fulfilment of prophecy depends on our obedience. Every prophetic word demands a response.

If the wind and the waves, if the fish in the sea, if demons, if sickness and even death itself all responded to the sound of His voice, how much more should we?

The Bible is full of examples of people who obeyed God and did what He was telling them to do.

Two of the most powerful and memorable are Joshua and the Israelites in Joshua 6 and the story of Gideon in the book of Judges.

In Joshua 6, God's people come to the great walled city of Jericho. This imposing fortress stands between them and their destiny, them and their promised land.

In a story that is familiar to us all, on the seventh day, God's people sound the trumpets and as the trumpet sounds God does a miracle. The walls fall down and God's people march in and claim a famous victory.

Obviously the walls didn't fall because of the volume of the trumpet playing. It was supernatural, divine intervention. Now God could have caused the walls to fall at any time, so why did He wait till the Israelites blew the trumpets? Because the sound of the trumpet was the sound of their obedience.

God had told His people to march around the city in silence for six days. On the seventh day they were to march around seven times, again in total silence. Only after the seventh circuit were they told to make a sound and blow the trumpet.

When God heard the sound of the trumpet blast, it was the sound of their obedience in doing what God had told them to. Their obedience could literally be heard. It was when God heard the sound of their obedience that He sprang into action and moved on their behalf.

The story of Gideon is a story of reluctant obedience to God. From an angelic visitation in a winepress to the famous "putting out the fleece", God takes this fearful man and turns him into a mighty warrior and judge who brings deliverance to Israel from the dreaded Midianites.

The story concludes with Gideon and his small army charging into the camp of the Midianites who had the overwhelmingly larger force.

As Israel marched into the camp, they produced a sound:

*"They blew their trumpets and broke the jars that were in their hands. The three companies blew the trumpets and smashed the jars. Grasping the torches in their left hands and holding in their right hands the trumpets they were to blow, they shouted, 'A sword for the Lord and for Gideon!' While each man held his position round the camp, all the Midianites ran, crying out as they fled.*
*When the three hundred trumpets sounded, the Lord caused the men throughout the camp to turn on each other with their swords." (Judges 7:19-22)*

As Gideon and his men obeyed God, they produced a sound – it was the sound of trumpets being blown, the sound of jars being smashed and the sound of God's people declaring who they served.

Like in Joshua 6, the obedience of God's people produced a sound. This sound once again caused God to step in as He confused the enemy into turning on each other.

It seems like our obedience to God is not just something that He sees, but something that He hears. An obedient life speaks to God. An obedient life produces a sound that heaven blesses. The sound of our obedience causes walls to fall, strongholds to be broken, our enemies to flee and the power of God to be unleashed in our circumstances.

In contrast to Joshua and Gideon there are plenty of stories in the Bible of people who disobeyed God.

One of these is King Saul. In 1 Samuel 15, the prophet Samuel told Saul that after defeating the Amalekites he had to destroy not only them but all their animals too. Saul half obeys God, but then he compromises. He spares some of the best of the sheep and cattle.

When confronted by Samuel, Saul initially denies it. But how is he found out? By a sound!

> *"But Samuel said, 'What then is this bleating of sheep in my ears? What is this lowing of cattle that I hear?" (1 Samuel 15:14)*

The sound of sheep led to Saul losing his kingdom! The sound of the sheep spoke of his disobedience and compromise and it would cost him everything.

It seems that our lives produce one of two sounds. One is the sound of obedience and the other is the sound of disobedience. The sound of obedience attracts God's presence and favour, while the sound of disobedience is an unpleasant sound in His ear and causes His presence and favour to be lifted from us. What sound is my life producing? Obedience or compromise? Is the sound of my life a pleasant sound in His ear or not?

## What is He saying?

Picture the scene, Mary Magdalene has gone to visit the tomb of Jesus, but his body is not there. Confused and broken hearted she breaks down weeping. Even a meeting with angels doesn't answer her question "where have they taken Jesus?"

Sensing someone standing behind her, Mary turns around and sees a man that she presumes is the gardener.

> "He asked her, 'Woman, why are you crying? Who is it you are looking for?'
>
> *Thinking He was the gardener, she said, 'Sir, if you have carried him away, tell me where you have put him, and I will get him.'*
>
> *Jesus said to her, 'Mary." (John 20:15-16)*

Mary would have been used to people saying her name. Every day people would have used her name. But when this man spoke her name, she knew who it was. Only one person spoke her name like that. Only one person sounded like that. She, by the sound of His voice, knows that it is Jesus.

> "He calls his own sheep by name and leads them out." (John 10:3)
>
> "I know my sheep and my sheep know me" (John 10:14)

She had heard that voice command seven demons to leave her. She had heard that voice speak peace into her troubled soul. She had heard that voice speak words of life to multitudes. She had heard that voice release words of blessing over children. She had heard that voice speak healing over sick bodies. Just three days earlier she had heard that voice from a cross cry, "It is finished".

No one sounded like Him. No other voice sounded so kind and yet so powerful, so gentle and yet so authoritative, so loving and yet so holy. Only the sound of His voice could produce both fear and awe, both worship and surrender.

Mary responded to the sound of His voice by doing this:

> *"She turned towards Him and cried out in Aramaic, 'Rabboni!' (which means 'Teacher').*
>
> *Jesus said, 'Do not hold on to Me, for I have not yet ascended to the Father. Go instead to My brothers and tell them, "I am ascending to My Father and your Father, to My God and your God."'*
>
> *Mary Magdalene went to the disciples with the news: 'I have seen the Lord!"*
> *(John 20:16-18)*

It is interesting that before she called Him "Lord", she first called Him "teacher". Lord is someone that you worship, teacher is someone that you follow.

A teacher guides, a teacher instructs, a teacher leads, a teacher shows the way. Her automatic response to His voice, is to call Him "teacher". She first knows Him as a teacher. As she knows Him as teacher, this in turn leads to knowing Him as Lord.

Jesus appears first to the one who recognises Him as teacher – the one who will listen to His instructions and do what He tells them. After she responds, what does He do? He gives her instructions! Characteristically, Mary obeys every single word.

How many today want to worship Him but don't want to be instructed by Him? How many today want to declare that He is Lord, but they don't want to listen to and obey His instructions? Only in obedience to His voice do we make Him truly Lord over our lives.

> *"Anyone who loves Me will obey my teaching. My Father will love them, and we will come to them and make our home with them." (John 14:23)*

In 1 Chronicles 14, David is in a dilemma. Does he fight against the Philistines or not? God tells David, wait and listen for the sound.

*"As soon as you hear the sound of marching in the tops of the poplar trees, move out to battle, because that will mean God has gone out in front of you to strike the Philistine army.' So, David did as God commanded him, and they struck down the Philistine army, all the way from Gibeon to Gezer." (v15-16)*

When you hear the sound – march. The sound was David's call to obey, his call to action, his call to battle.

What is the sound of heaven telling you to do? Can you hear the sound from the tops of the trees? Is it calling you to give, calling you to go, calling you to repent, calling you to pray, calling you to serve?

We have to know what it is to hear clearly what God is telling us and then respond to that sound.

God's promise to David was that as he went, God had already gone ahead of him, guaranteeing his victory.

When we obey God, we have the assurance that He has already gone ahead of us wherever He is telling us to go. The shepherd goes ahead of the sheep. His voice draws them into places He has already been.

His voice pulls you into where He is. Obedience brings you into alignment not only with His will but into His presence.

It is time to hear and respond to the voice of God. The trumpets are sounding, and the lion is roaring. He is calling His people to battle; He is calling them into action. It is calling to pray, a call to go, a call to follow. Will you respond to heaven's sound?

*"They will follow the Lord; He will roar like a lion. When He roars, His children will come trembling from the west" (Hosea 11:10)*

# THE SOUND OF THE CHURCH

*"The wind blows wherever it pleases. You hear its sound, but you cannot tell where it comes from or where it is going. So it is with everyone born of the Spirit."*
*(John 3:8)*

In this scripture in John 3, Jesus speaks about one of the great mysteries of the spirit realm. Beginning by talking of the wind, Jesus shares how no one knows the source of the wind or its direction, but everyone can hear its sound. This could be the sound of the wind itself or more likely the sound of the environment that is affected by the wind. Wherever the wind blows there is a sound that is created. This could be the sound of trees rustling in a gentle breeze or the frightening sounds that are produced by fierce gales or hurricanes. But, where the wind is really blowing, there will always be a sound that is produced.

Jesus then takes this parable from nature and He compares it to people who are born of the Holy Spirit. He says that people who are born again, made new by the power of the Spirit, they too will create a sound. Wherever they go, their life will produce a sound that will affect their environment.

"So it is" – Jesus is speaking very matter-of-factly here. We don't realise the effect that our lives are having, but every one of us produces a sound. The Church of

Jesus, whether that be us as individuals or the Church as a corporate body – it produces a sound. A sound that cannot be denied or dismissed. A Church that is filled with the Spirit, led by the Spirit and empowered by the Spirit creates a sound of hope and healing that can transform cultures and change nations.

## What sound are you producing?

I recently asked my followers on social media if they had a favourite sound. The replies were interesting and diverse. Rain and waterfalls. Children laughing. Birds chirping. Coffee machines! We all have sounds that immediately create an emotion within us. Pleasant sounds can produce peace, security and joy or can cause us to be reminded of certain precious memories. It's incredible the change in mood or atmosphere that a certain sound can produce.

On the flip side we all have those sounds that are irritating, annoying or simply unpleasant. They can disturb our peace or even bring great distress.

Every person on this planet has their own sound. Have you ever had someone walk into a room and immediately the atmosphere changes? Sometimes they don't need to say a thing. They carry an aura; they emit a certain sound. Some people enter a room and the room feels warmer or more joyful. Some people bring a calmness or a stability to a situation just by being there.

In contrast some people carry an unpleasant "sound". They enter a room and it's like they carry a heaviness or a depressive spirit that effects all those around them. Some people just enter a room full of people and immediately you can feel the stress or the tension rise. They may not have said or done anything, but you can almost feel the negative sound waves emit from their lives.

What sound is my life producing? It's a great question to ask!
Likewise, every church has its own unique sound.

Other words for this would be "culture" or "atmosphere" but for the purpose of this book I am using the word "sound" because I feel that to be a more Biblical term. Every church has its own unique culture, atmosphere or sound. It's usually the first thing you notice when you enter the building. The sound of a place is not always something you can put your finger on or define, but it's something very noticeable and very powerful.

In Acts 2 we read of three sounds. The first is the sound that comes from heaven. The mighty rushing wind of the Holy Spirit.

*"Suddenly a sound like the blowing of a violent wind came from heaven and filled the whole house where they were sitting" (v2)*

The third sound is the sound of salvation as around three thousand people were baptised and born again.

But in between these two sounds was another sound. It was the sound of the Church.

*"All of them were filled with the Holy Spirit and began to speak in other tongues as the Spirit enabled them." (v4)*

What happened was that the source of the sound from heaven, the Holy Spirit, came and filled these 120 believers. The result was that these 120 believers began to produce their own sound from heaven, a supernatural sound coming from the Holy Spirit.

Notice what happened in the city.

*"Now there were staying in Jerusalem God-fearing Jews from every nation under heaven. When they heard this sound, a crowd came together in bewilderment, because each one heard their own language being spoken. Utterly amazed, they asked: 'Aren't all these who are speaking Galileans? Then how is it that each of us hears them in our native language?" (v5-8)*

*"Amazed and perplexed, they asked one another, 'What does this mean?" (v12)*

"When they heard this sound.." What sound? Not the sound of the mighty rushing wind, but the sound of the Church! The Spirit-filled, Spirit-empowered Church produced a sound that shook the city! The sound that they produced was so noticeable that it opened their hearts to the message of the gospel.

This is what happens when a church releases the sound of heaven! It shakes cities, it transforms atmospheres, it changes lives!

I believe one of the greatest questions that we can ask if we want to reach our communities is this – What sound do we as a church produce? I believe one of the most powerful things that we can do to transform our churches is to change our sound, our culture, our atmosphere.

Many times, churches think that they can change things by changing the programme or changing the building décor or changing other external things. We don't realise none of these things attract the lost. The lost are always attracted by our "sound". It is always the sound that we produce that gets the attention of a city.

I have been in churches that externally seem to have it all together, but there is something not quite right. Their sound is a little off key.

Division has a sound.

Religious control has a sound.

Apathy has a sound.

Compromise has a sound.

These are awful sounds that will repel everyone. Sometimes you can visit these churches and wonder why people still attend. But they are so used to these sounds that they have become numb to them. And they wonder why people are not getting saved. They wonder why they aren't growing. Their sound isn't right.

Some churches just sound old. This isn't a debate about traditional vs contemporary. They are external style issues. Some churches just sound stale. They have a staleness in their worship and a staleness in their preaching. This is often because they are living on yesterday's manna, living off of the sound of a previous season. But then there are prophetic churches that are listening to what heaven is doing now. There is a prophetic sharpness to their vision, a prophetic flow in their worship and a prophetic unction in their preaching. They are all about hearing and responding to what heaven is doing and saying now. They are living in the now of God. Living in the Rhema of the Spirit. These kinds of churches are making a new sound and a new song. There is a freshness, a life, an energy pulsating through them that you can feel. It's alive, it's attractive, it's contagious!

Our churches have to produce the sounds of heaven.

One of the sounds of heaven is unity.

In 2 Chronicles 5 we read of the dedication of the temple:

*"The trumpeters and musicians joined in unison to give praise and thanks to the Lord. Accompanied by trumpets, cymbals and other instruments, the singers raised their voices in praise to the Lord and sang: "He is good; His love endures forever." Then the temple of the Lord was filled with the cloud" (v13)*

The emphasis in this verse is on their unity. They sung with one voice, they played in unison. This is not a comment on their musical ability. This is a comment on their heart posture. There was a unity and a collectiveness in their praise. Just as in Acts 2, they were not just in one place, but they were together in one place.

Their unity was a pleasant sound that reached heaven. Psalm 133 talks about now the sound of our unity is good and pleasing in the ears of God. The result in 2 Chronicles 5 is that the glory of the Lord filled the temple (v14)

Heaven responded to the sound of their unity and the glory of the Lord filled their gathering.

Churches that are full of division, cliques, criticism, back-biting, unforgiveness, jealousy and competition create a sound that is offensive to God and abhorrent to the lost.

But churches where there is true love, unity, honour, forgiveness, putting others first – they create a sound that attracts the glory of God, commands the blessing of

God and is attractive to outsiders.

In 1 Corinthians 13 Paul talks about a church where there is an absence of love. He says that no matter what this church does or how spiritual it may appear; it produces a sound that is like a "resounding gong or a clanging cymbal" (v1). It is an unpleasant sound, an empty sound, a lifeless sound.

In contrast when there is peace it keeps us in tune with each other (Colossians 3:17 – The Message). There is something about a loving, united church where we truly care for each other and love each other and want the best for each that just sounds so good!

It's interesting that the word 'harmony' can be a musical term but can also speak of people in one accord. But the result is the same in both cases. It's a pleasing sound, a delightful sound.

The sound that our churches produce is so important. Our reputation goes before us. Our atmosphere is the first thing people notice. People will hear us before they see us.

Passion has a sound. Faith has a sound. Hope has a sound. Expectancy has a sound.

There are some churches that in everything – the preaching, the music, the conversations, the lives of its members – you can hear passion, you can hear faith, you can hear hope, you can hear expectancy.

One of the greatest sounds of the Kingdom is joy!

*"Make a joyful noise unto the Lord, all the earth: make a loud noise, and rejoice, and sing praise.*
*Sing unto the Lord with the harp; with the harp, and the voice of a psalm.*
*With trumpets and sound of cornet make a joyful noise before the Lord, the King."*
*(Psalm 98:4-6 – KJV)*

Some churches just sound joyful! They create a joyful noise. There is no sound that is more attractive or life giving. A joyful noise literally has the power to bring healing to people's souls and bodies.

The miraculous has a sound! There are many scriptures we could use but one of my favourites is the healing of the cripple in Acts 3-4. As this man stands before a sceptical crowd they are rendered speechless:

*"But since they could see the man who had been healed standing there with them, there was nothing they could say." (Acts 4:14)*

Signs and wonders have a language all of their own. The man's healing spoke louder than a hundred sermons. This man's healed body spoke of the power of the resurrected Jesus! You cannot argue with a miracle!

Imagine how our cities would react when the sound of the miraculous is once again heard in our churches! Empty wheelchairs, X-Rays that show tumours disappearing – they shout louder than unbelief and cynicism! One of my pastor friends says, "Healing is God's dinner bell for salvation!"

The prophetic has a sound. Paul writes about what happens when an unbeliever enters a church and hears the sound of the prophetic:

*"But if an unbeliever or an enquirer comes in while everyone is prophesying, they are convicted of sin and are brought under judgment by all, as the secrets of their hearts are laid bare. So they will fall down and worship God, exclaiming, 'God is really among you!" (1 Corinthians 14:24-25)*

There is nothing more glorious than being in a church that sounds like heaven!

Sadly, I have been in many churches where there is no sound of life, of passion, of expectancy, of faith, of joy. The sounds of the prophetic and the sounds of the miraculous are absent.

### Releasing heaven's sound

How do we change the "sound" of our church? Placing the right people in right leadership positions is an important step. Important conversations and strategic decision-making can all be key to changing the "sound" or "culture" of a church.

But ultimately the source of heaven's sound is the Holy Spirit. Those who are born of the Spirit create heaven's sound (John 3:8). It was as the disciples in the Upper Room were filled with the One who sounded like a mighty rushing wind that they made a sound, as the "Spirit enabled them" (Acts 2:4).

What we desperately need is to allow the sound of the mighty rushing wind to be heard in our churches! We need to allow the Spirit of God to be free to move in power and to bring life and to bring heaven's sound! Each of us need to be filled with the Spirit, empowered by the Spirit and led by the Spirit.

It is as the Spirit fills His people that the sound of heaven will be heard in our churches. This sound cannot be contained within the four walls of the church!

Heaven's sound shakes cities and transforms atmospheres. It is a sound that attracts the lost, changes lives and sets the captives free!

For each one of us as individuals our lives produce a song that can change rooms!

Imagine what it would look like if every one of us went into our workplaces, our schools, into the homes of our neighbours and we carried heaven's sound?

There is an incredible account in Luke 1 of Mary, pregnant with Jesus, entering the home of Elizabeth, who is pregnant with John the Baptist. As Mary enters the home, she greets Elizabeth and something supernatural takes place.

> "When Elizabeth heard Mary's greeting, the baby leaped in her womb, and Elizabeth was filled with the Holy Spirit." (v41)

How could a simple greeting cause an unborn baby to leap and a woman to be filled with the Holy Spirit?

> "As soon as the sound of your greeting reached my ears, the baby in my womb leaped for joy." (v44)

When you carry the presence of Jesus even your greeting produces a supernatural sound that causes others to leap with excitement and encounter the Holy Spirit!

This is how heaven invades a city! When every member of the Church is so full of His presence that wherever we go we carry a supernatural sound. Now even common, ordinary things like saying "hello" to someone carries a sound that is supercharged with the power of the Holy Spirit! It is heaven's sound flowing out of us that changes the lives of those we come into contact with.

## The healing power of sound

The following is taken from a secular website:

*One of the most amazing experiments on the power of sound was conducted by Doctor Masaru Emoto. Dr. Emoto, a graduate of the Yokohama Municipal University's Department of Humanities and Sciences and the author of the bestselling book Messages from Water, gained worldwide acclaim for his ground-breaking research and his discovery that water is affected by vibrational sound in some very surprising ways.*

*In his experiments, Dr. Emoto analysed the formation of differently shaped crystals in water as it was exposed to different sounds in different forms. Part of his research included verbal affirmations, thoughts, music, and even prayers from a priest. He focused on verbal affirmations of love and gratitude as they were being directed toward water that was sitting in a Petri dish. He then analysed the water under a microscope and took before and after pictures to document the change.*

*Dr. Emoto and his team observed that after the experiment very beautiful crystals had formed in some of the frozen water samples where the positive vibrational waves were directed. Dr. Emoto then exposed water samples to music from Mozart, Beethoven, and other classical composers and found that beautiful crystal shapes formed in these samples as well.*

*He also experimented with people saying things like "you fool," "I will kill you," and other unpleasant phrases using a harsh tone. Dr. Emoto found that ugly, incomplete, and malformed crystals were formed in the water samples exposed to these negative expressions and tones.*

*Dr. Emoto concluded that any sound is vibration, and vibrations such as music and other positive sounds including the human voice can be a form of healing energy. His research also showed that thoughts emit vibrations at frequencies we can't yet precisely determine, and that they too have the power to heal.*

*In nature, vibrations travel via water and air. This is significant when you consider the human body is approximately 65 percent water. What vibrations or sounds are we communicating to one another, and what sort of energy are we producing for ourselves and for the rest of humanity?*

*Sound is a potent, powerful energy that can express love and concern, or cause great pain and destruction. Human consciousness has begun to accept the possibility that we live in a magical world where the powerful energy vibrations made by music, positive thoughts, and words of love and harmony produce peace and beauty while vibrations lacking this positive energy produce distortion. Even the American Cancer Society has acknowledged that certain types of meditation such as the ones using a repetition of mantras–either silently in the form of thoughts or out loud–can bring a response of relaxation in the body.*

© https://chopra.com/articles/the-healing-power-of-sound

Isn't it fascinating that non-believers have worked out that certain sounds can produce a healing effect on the human body and soul? We know that advertisers, composers, musicians will create sounds that in turn create certain emotions – feelings of romance, fear, excitement, tranquillity, danger.

If this is true of natural sounds, how much more powerful are the sounds that are produced by lovers of God, filled with the Holy Spirit?

In 1 Samuel 16 Saul, king of Israel, is tormented by an evil spirit. The Bible records how young David, the man after God's own heart enters Saul's service and plays music whenever the evil spirit comes to torment Saul.

*"Whenever the spirit from God came on Saul, David would take up his lyre and play. Then relief would come to Saul; he would feel better, and the evil spirit would leave him." (v23)*

This is the power of heaven's sound! When a lover of God releases heaven's sound it has the power to bring relief to the tormented and deliverance to the captives.

Around us every day are those tormented by satan. They are waiting for men and women, full of the Spirit who carry and release the sound of heaven wherever they go. Contained within that sound is peace, freedom and the power to break the chains of oppression.

When we talk about releasing heaven's sound it is important to realise that this is more than just music. I am not suggesting you take a guitar into your office and start playing hymns whilst people are trying to work!

No, your love creates a sound. Mercy creates a sound. Forgiveness creates a sound. Honour creates a sound. Humility creates a sound. Servanthood creates a sound. Integrity creates a sound. Your testimony creates a sound.

When you are filled with the Spirit, everything you do emanates with the sound of heaven. It is that sound that causes darkness to flee and yokes to be lifted!

Staying with King Saul, there is a more positive story about him in 1 Samuel 10. This is before he is anointed king and speaks of a powerful encounter he had with the Spirit of God. The prophet Samuel foretells what will happen to him:

*"As you approach the town, you will meet a procession of prophets coming down from the high place with lyres, tambourines, pipes and harps being played before them, and they will be prophesying. The Spirit of the Lord will come powerfully upon you, and you will prophesy with them; and you will be changed into a different person." (1 Samuel 10:5-6)*

I love this image of the prophets coming down from the high place and creating this sound of praise that is both prophetic and powerful.

As Saul gets among them and this sound is all around him, the Spirit of God comes upon him in power and transforms him into a different person!

This is a wonderful picture of the prophetic church! God is looking for a company that have been in the high places. They have been in the presence of the Lord! In that place they have heard the sound of the Spirit and now they come down into the valley, to the needy and the broken, and they are creating a sound from heaven. They are creating a sound that is supernatural and pregnant with the life of God! When the world then gets among that sound, something happens to them! A change, a transformation takes place, by encountering this sound, the presence of God can bring transformation and breakthrough to all who hear it.

## The sound of rain

Several years ago, I visited Argentina for the first time. One of the places I visited was a town called Chancani. Meaning "the end of the road", Chancani is an incredibly remote, very isolated community where there was very little Christian presence and a real spiritual darkness caused by the enemy.

When we arrived, Chancani had been in a drought that had lasted several months. I was there for one night and God did some wonderful things, saving a precious couple that have gone on to have a wonderful ministry in that town and healing a woman who had been born deaf and mute!

One of the most remarkable things that took place was when the service ended and I got into the vehicle that was taking me back to our accommodation. As soon as I shut the car door, there was a huge crack of thunder and the heavens opened and began to pour with rain.

That night lying in bed I heard the sound of rain pelting down on the tin roof as God ended the drought. A few years later when I went back to Chancani I was told, "Before you came here, it never rained! Now it rains all the time!"

A few months after this I was in Albania during the month of August. This is the hottest month of the year. During August they won't get a drop of rain. The first afternoon we were there we went into the city centre and the sun was baking down, the sky was blue and there was not a cloud in the sky. We began to talk about our upcoming conference, "Times of Refreshing". As we spoke, we looked up into the cloudless sky amazed as rain began to fall where we were, refreshing us for several minutes before ending as suddenly as it began.

Sometime after this I went to the nation of Mexico. On the first night I was preaching in a sports auditorium. It had been a warm sunny day with no bad weather forecast.

I preached the gospel and invited people to the altar who wanted to give their lives to Jesus. The moment the first person responded, the heavens opened and we heard the sound of rain pelting down on the roof so hard that it drowned out the sound of the people praying. This lasted till we had finished ministering to the last person and then the rain stopped. Remarkably this same phenomenon took place each night as we ministered in Mexico.

It has become something of a joke among team members that have been on several missions with me that, wherever we go, we bring the sound of rain!

In a dry and arid land or in a community that relies on agriculture, the sound of rain contains within it life and the hope of a future harvest.

I believe we are called to be rain makers. To go into dry and barren communities, to go to people that are lost and have no hope and to bring the sound of rain, the sound of life, the sound of hope and the sound of the good news of Jesus.

I believe God is calling us to fall in love with our communities. I visit many places where the believers speak so negatively over their community. They tell you everything the devil is doing, all the problems that are taking place and how hopeless things are. They are literally prophesying a sound of death over their city.

When we fall in love with our communities, we begin to sing a love song over them! We sing a song of hope, a song of freedom, a song of healing. Contained within that song is a sound from heaven that contains the rains of revival. Heavens song has the power to set addicts free, restore the broken, save the lost, heal the sick and transform the most hopeless and the most desperate.

Let us spend time in His Presence and be filled with His Spirit. And then let's go and release heaven's sound wherever we go. Let us be that sound of hope, that sound of change, that sound of revival! I hear the sound of an abundance of rain!

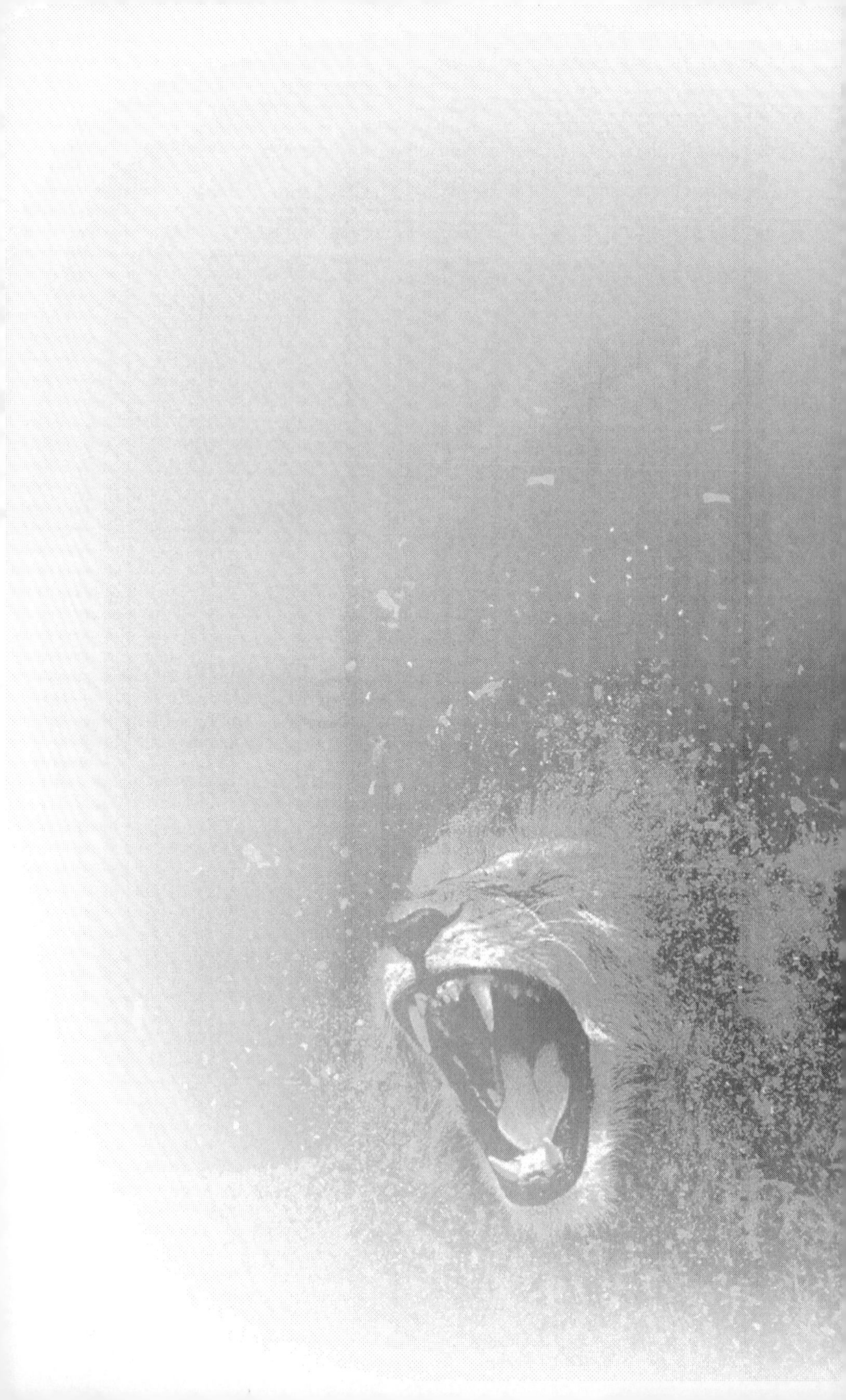

# CONCLUSION: FINDING YOUR PENGUIN

Judges chapter 12 tells the strange story of the killing of forty two thousand Ephraimites who were betrayed by a sound. Apparently the tribe of Ephraim couldn't pronounce the word "Shibboleth" properly and when the opposing tribes met a stranger on the road they simply asked them to repeat this word. When an Ephraimite failed to do this, their identity was exposed and they were killed.

I find it fascinating that they could tell who belonged to which tribe by the sound that they either could or couldn't make.

I believe that within the heart of every person on the planet is a desire to belong, a need for community, a longing for family. What we are really looking for is a tribe that makes the same sound as us, a people group who make the same noise, speak the same language and whose heart beats in time with ours.

In the animated movie Happy Feet, a take on the mating ritual of penguins is shown. In the film, every emperor penguin sings a unique song called a "heart-song" to attract a mate. If the male penguin's heart-song matches the female's song, the two penguins mate.

There is nothing more fulfilling than finding someone who has the same heart-song as yours. I believe not only is this true in a romantic relationship but I believe it is also true in the context of the church that we call our spiritual home.

There can be nothing more frustrating than trying to be planted in a church and yet you are the only one who can't say "Shibboleth". You love them, you try your best to support and yet they don't make the same sound as you. Your heart-songs don't match.

But I can tell you that there is something joyful about walking into a place and knowing – my song matches theirs! I can't put my finger on it, but I recognise their sound – it's the same one that is beating in my own heart too. Of course there can still be times when we clash, when one of us is out of tune with the other – but when you know that this is a place I can belong, I can flourish, I can grow, I like the sound that they are producing, then there is nothing more glorious.

This is a word for the misfits – for those who have always struggled to belong. Please don't get discouraged and quit fellowshipping. Neither become a restless wanderer moving from one place to the other. I believe this: God has a penguin for you! He has a tribe for you that sings the same song that is in your heart. Ask God to lead you to your tribe, to your penguin.

Whether it is a church family, a friendship group or a spouse – God has a penguin for everyone. When you find yours – value it, treasure it, look after it. Nothing is more precious or satisfying than knowing that you have found where you belong.

Our ultimate penguin is Jesus Christ! No human love can satisfy like His love. He is the One that we were created for relationship with. He is the One that satisfies like no other. In Song of Songs, the beloved describes her heart as pounding for the one she loves (2:4). At the same time He is knocking on the door, longing to come in and be with her (v2). The sound of Him knocking on the door beats in perfect timing with the pounding of her heart. Oh, how His love is truly the only thing that can satisfy, the only thing that can bring meaning, the only thing that brings purpose to us. His love brings satisfaction, His love brings joy, His love makes us complete. He is truly our penguin – the One our soul longs for. Our heart longs for Him and His heart longs for us. When these two hearts beat in time with each other, when we are one with Him and He is one with us, we have found life itself.

"Are you tired? Worn out? Burned out on religion? Come to Me. Get away with Me and you'll recover your life. I'll show you how to take a real rest. Walk with Me and work with Me—watch how I do it. Learn the unforced rhythms of grace. I won't lay anything heavy or ill-fitting on you. Keep company with Me and you'll learn to live freely and lightly." (Matthew 11:28-30 – The Message)

Life in our own strength, a life of busyness, of trying to keep up with the Jones', of being on the treadmill of our daily routine – all it leads is to stress, burn out and exhaustion.

But there is an invitation to walk with Him, to lean in and listen to His sound, to live a life of intimacy and communion with Him. This is the unforced rhythms of grace – when our lives walk in time with His, when our hearts beat as one with His. This is joy, this is peace, this is rest.

"God's timing" – it is less about seconds and minutes and hours as it is about rhythm, relationship and one-ness. Jesus is God's perfect will, He is always on time and He invites us into a place of One-ness with Him where He lives His life and purposes out through me. When I try and live life at my own pace, I know I can easily go off track. But when He becomes my Divine Conductor, when I yield to Him and find my rest in Him, I am always in a place of contentment.

We need to find a place where all other noises are drowned out and I am listening to Him, letting Him lead, guide and work through me.

I find that when I am one with Him there are times of incredible activity and yet I am never burnt out and also times of no activity and yet I am never bored. When I live with Him as the metronome of my life, I live in a place of perfect contentment. It is only when my heart is somehow beating to a different pace to His that stress and burn out comes.

The revivalist John G Lakes' grandson said, "My grandfather had the knack of always being exactly where God wanted him at just the right time".

This is the unforced rhythms of grace. This is what it means to have a heart that beats in time with heaven. This only comes through times of being alone with Him, being still and listening.

Lean in. Listen. Respond. Then you can truly live.

"O God! Thou hast made us for Thyself and our souls are restless, searching, until they find their rest in Thee" – Saint Augustine

# AFTERWORD: THE POWER OF SPEAKING IN TONGUES

*"All of them were filled with the Holy Spirit and began to speak in other tongues as the Spirit enabled them." (Acts 2:4)*

I recently caused a stir with some of my followers on social media after I put up a post, challenging worship leaders to encourage church members to sing in tongues during our corporate praise times.

Whilst many agreed with me some argued back at me with the two main points of contention being as follows:

- If people are to speak or sing in tongues in a church service, it should always be followed by an interpretation

- God has not chosen to give every person the gift of tongues

It seems to me that as I read the New Testament there are two uses of the gift of "tongues" and sometimes we can confuse the two. Failure to see the difference can result in a wrong understanding, as demonstrated by some of the criticism I received following my post.

## The first use of tongues

In 1 Corinthians 12, the Apostle Paul gives a list of nine supernatural gifts that the Holy Spirit has made available to the Body of Christ. These are known as the "gifts of the Spirit" and are listed below:

*"To one there is given through the Spirit a message of wisdom, to another a message of knowledge by means of the same Spirit, to another faith by the same Spirit, to another gifts of healing by that one Spirit, to another miraculous powers, to another prophecy, to another distinguishing between spirits, to another speaking in different kinds of tongues, and to still another the interpretation of tongues." (v8-10)*

As you can see, one of the gifts mentioned is the gift of "speaking in different kinds of tongues" and another is "the interpretation of tongues". It is worth pointing out that the word "tongues" is better translated as "languages". Indeed, if you look in the New Testament it seems that when people spoke in tongues, it was another earthly language (rather than a heavenly language), albeit one that they were able to speak supernaturally (i.e. not something that they had learned at school).

My understanding of the spiritual gift of speaking in tongues mentioned in 1 Corinthians 12:10-11 is that it is referring to the giving of a prophetic word or message in an unknown or unlearned language.

Church services two thousand years ago were much different to church services today. Today many Christians find themselves as spectators, sitting and listening as one or two people minister from behind a pulpit. But for the early church, everyone was encouraged to take part. Someone would bring a song, someone else would bring a teaching, someone else would bring a prophetic word etc.

It seems that sometimes prophetic words were given in the known language of the day and could be understood by everybody. But it also seems that sometimes a prophetic message would be brought in an unknown language, as the bringer of the message was inspired by the Holy Spirit. This message in tongues would then be translated supernaturally by someone else who would give the interpretation in a way that everyone could understand (1 Corinthians 14:26)

Throughout Church history, and still today, I have heard wonderful testimonies of people giving prophetic messages in tongues and God speaking powerfully through the interpretation. These are spiritual gifts that should be desired by all (1 Corinthians 14:1) and can be powerfully used to strengthen the local church (v26).

Paul, however, does put some guidelines in place for the use of giving messages in tongues in church services.

Firstly, Paul seems to indicate that not everyone will move in this gift (1 Corinthians 12:30). Secondly, Paul said that messages in tongues should be limited to two or three in a public gathering (1 Corinthians 14:27). Messages in tongues should be given one after the other, rather than everyone speaking at the same time and they should always be followed by an interpretation (v27). Finally, Paul suggests that giving messages in tongues is perhaps not wise when unbelievers are present (v23).

Paul himself says that he preferred not to give messages in tongues but rather preferred to prophesy in the known language of the day (v19) and he encouraged those that did give messages in tongues to "cut out the middle man" as it were and mature to the greater gift of giving a prophetic word that everyone can understand (v5).

So, this is one use of the gift of tongues in the New Testament – the giving of a prophetic word in a public gathering in an unknown language, as led by the Holy Spirit.

## The second use of tongues

I want us to look now at the second use of tongues in the New Testament. This is the use of tongues as a prayer language and, as we will see, this is very different to what we have already looked at.

In the book of Acts there are three occasions when people are recorded as speaking in tongues. Let's read all three.

The first is the disciples on the Day of Pentecost:

> *"All of them were filled with the Holy Spirit and began to speak in other tongues as the Spirit enabled them." (Acts 2:4)*

The second is the household of Cornelius:
> *"While Peter was still speaking these words, the Holy Spirit came on all who heard the message. The circumcised believers who had come with Peter were astonished that the gift of the Holy Spirit had been poured out even on Gentiles. For they heard them speaking in tongues and praising God." (Acts 10:44-46)*

The third occasion is a group of men that Paul encounters in Ephesus:

> *"When Paul placed his hands on them, the Holy Spirit came on them, and they spoke in tongues and prophesied." (Acts 19:6)*

I want us to notice three things that are very important:

1. This was something that they all did. On all three occasions, the Holy Spirit came on groups of people and all of them without exception spoke in tongues. This would indicate that this use of tongues is something that is available for every Christian.

2. They all spoke in tongues at the same time. This use of tongues was used as part of their corporate prayer and praise time.

3. There was no interpretation given. This use of tongues was not them giving a prophetic word to the church, that then needed to be explained, rather this was them speaking and singing to God, using tongues as a prayer language rather than another way of moving in the prophetic.

Although Paul seems to have rarely given messages in tongues in public meetings, speaking and singing in tongues as part of his prayer life was something that he did all the time! He boasted in 1 Corinthians 14:18 that he spoke in tongues more than any of them!

Paul is not the only Christian to love speaking in tongues as part of their walk with Jesus. David Yonggi Cho, leader of the world's largest church said:

"As a young Christian I could not see the importance of tongues in my Christian life. However, the longer I believe in Jesus, the more I feel the tremendous importance of tongues in my own personal Christian life. I spend a good deal of my prayer life praying in my spiritual language. Sometimes I feel a burden of prayer, yet I know not exactly what I should pray for, or I may not have the words to express what I feel. This is the time I enter my spiritual language and pierce through my natural ability to articulate to God what I am feeling. I can go directly into my Father's presence through the Holy Spirit"

Smith Wigglesworth, the great Pentecostal evangelist said:

"No Pentecostal person ought to get out of bed without being lost in the Spirit and speaking in tongues as the Spirit gives utterance" - Smith Wigglesworth

John G Lake, the great apostolic missionary who saw phenomenal signs and wonders declared, "Tongues has been the making of my ministry".

## Praying in tongues

Discussing his own prayer life, Paul differentiates between what he calls praying with his mind and praying with his spirit.

*"For if I pray in a tongue, my spirit prays, but my mind is unfruitful. So what shall I do? I will pray with my spirit, but I will also pray with my understanding."*
*(1 Corinthians 14:14-15).*

Paul says that there are times when he prays with his mind. This means that the source of his prayer his mind (that has been renewed to become the mind of Christ), and he is praying using his own native language, using words that he can understand as he prays about whatever he is thinking about at that particular moment.

Paul says this kind of praying is good.

However, there are times when Paul prays, not in his own language but in a language supernaturally given to him by the Holy Spirit. In that moment he has no idea what he is actually saying. Paul describes this kind of prayer as "praying with my spirit". In other words, the source of his prayer is not his mind, but it comes from a deeper place within him: his spirit, the part of him that is communicating directly to God.

Paul says that this kind of prayer is not to man but to God (v2). Although all prayer is of course to God, the indication seems to be that praying in tongues is a more intimate form of prayer. It is spirit communicating directly to Spirit, deep calling unto deep.

The Message translation puts it like this:

> "I'm grateful to God for the gift of praying in tongues that He gives us for praising Him, which leads to wonderful intimacies we enjoy with Him."
> *(1 Corinthians 14:18 – The Mess)*

In Romans 8, Paul talks about the problem we can sometimes have in prayer when we only pray using our minds.

Of course, many times we know what we should pray for and how we should pray, however there are also many times when we don't know what to pray for or how we should pray. Sometimes we may know what to pray for, but we don't have the words to express our desires. Sometimes our own minds can actually be hostile to God's will as we try and pray our own will into a situation (v6). It is on these occasions, that we need to bypass our minds and allow the Holy Spirit to "intercede for us with groans that words cannot express" (v26).

Do you ever feel a burden to pray but are unsure what you should pray for? Pray in tongues.

Do you ever want to pray about something but are unsure how you should pray? Pray in tongues.

Do you ever want to pray about a situation, but you want to make sure that it is God's will that you are praying and not your own? Pray in tongues.

Do you ever run out of words in prayer or struggle to express your prayer to God? Pray in tongues.

When you pray in tongues you are praying in perfect agreement with God's character, God's desires and God's purposes.

In Corinthians 14:2 Paul writes:

*"For anyone who speaks in a tongue does not speak to people but to God. Indeed, no one understands them; they utter mysteries by the Spirit."*

When you pray in tongues you are praying a mystery by the Holy Spirit. The word mystery can be translated as a sacred mystery or a secret.

There are many things in this life that we just don't know about. There is a spiritual reality that is unseen, and we are often unaware of. We often don't know what satan is up to or what God is up to for that matter. When we pray in tongues, we are praying about things that are happening in the unseen spiritual realm. We are praying about things that may be hidden to us in the natural. When we pray in tongues, we are being set free from the limitations of our minds and understanding. When we are praying in tongues, we are praying about God's invisible Heavenly Kingdom and calling it to be made manifest in the seen realm.

Earlier in 1 Corinthians, Paul says:

*"This is what we speak, not in words taught us by human wisdom but in words taught by the Spirit, explaining spiritual realities with Spirit-taught words." (2:13)*

When we pray in tongues, we are not praying according to human wisdom, but we are praying according to the leading of the Holy Spirit. God's wisdom appears foolish to man, that is why sometimes praying in tongues can seem childish and why it is often mocked by unbelievers. But when we pray in tongues, we are releasing God's wisdom, as taught by the Holy Spirit into a situation.

The following is an article from the New York Times from 2006

*Researchers at the University of Pennsylvania took brain images of five women while they spoke in tongues and found that their frontal lobes – the thinking, wilful part of the brain through which people control what they do – were relatively quiet, as were the language centres. The regions involved in maintaining self-consciousness* were active. The women were not in blind trances, and it was unclear which region was driving the behaviour.

The images, appearing in the current issue of the journal Psychiatry Research: Neuroimaging, pinpoint the most active areas of the brain. The images are the first of their kind taken during this spoken religious practice, which has roots in the Old and New Testaments and in Pentecostal churches established in the early 1900s. The women in the study were healthy, active churchgoers.

"The amazing thing was how the images supported people's interpretation of what was happening," said Dr. Andrew B. Newberg, leader of the study team, which included Donna Morgan, Nancy Wintering and Mark Waldman. "The way they describe it, and what they believe, is that God is talking through them," he said. Dr. Newberg is also a co-author of "Why We Believe What We Believe."

In the study, the researchers used imaging techniques to track changes in blood flow in each woman's brain in two conditions, once as she sang a gospel song and again while speaking in tongues. By comparing the patterns created by these two emotional, devotional activities, the researchers could pinpoint blood-flow peaks and valleys unique to speaking in tongues.

Ms. Morgan, a co-author of the study, was also a research subject. She is a born-again Christian who says she considers the ability to speak in tongues a gift. "You're aware of your surroundings," she said. "You're not really out of control. But you have no control over what's happening. You're just flowing. You're in a realm of peace and comfort, and it's a fantastic feeling."

Contrary to what may be a common perception, studies suggest that people who *speak in tongues rarely suffer from mental problems. A recent study of nearly 1,000 evangelical Christians in England found that those who engaged in the practice were more emotionally stable than those who did not. Researchers have identified at least two forms of the practice, one ecstatic and frenzied, the other subdued and nearly silent.*

*The new findings contrasted sharply with images taken of other spiritually inspired mental states like meditation, which is often a highly focused mental exercise, activating the frontal lobes.*

*The scans also showed a dip in the activity of a region called the left caudate. "The findings from the frontal lobes are very clear, and make sense, but the caudate is usually active when you have positive affect, pleasure, positive emotions," said Dr. James A. Coan, a psychologist at the University of Virginia. "So, it's not so clear what that finding says" about speaking in tongues.*

*The caudate area is also involved in motor and emotional control, Dr. Newberg said, so it may be that practitioners, while mindful of their circumstances, nonetheless cede some control over their bodies and emotions.*

© https://www.nytimes.com/2006/11/07/health/07brain.html

In Ephesians 6, Paul tells us about the battle that all of us are engaged in every day. This battle is not "against flesh and blood, but against the rulers, against the authorities, against the powers of this dark world and against the spiritual forces of evil in the heavenly realms" (v12)

As well as taking up the armour of God, Paul concludes this passage by telling us another way that we can stay strong against the devil's schemes:

*"Pray in the Spirit on all occasions with all kinds of prayers and requests." (v18).*

Prayer in the Spirit is how we fight against the enemy. Although it could be argued that praying in the Spirit involves more than just praying in tongues, tongues is very much the context used when Paul describes praying in the spirit in 1 Corinthians 14. It seems that when I pray in tongues, I am releasing a supernatural power and authority that gives me victory over the enemy. I strongly believe that praying in tongues can give victory against depression, sickness, anxiety, fear, doubt or whatever else the enemy is attacking me with.

## Praising with tongues

In the same way that tongues is a powerful way to pray to God, it is also a powerful way that we can praise Him too.

*"I will sing with my spirit, but I will also sing with my understanding"*
*(1 Corinthians 14:15)*

Although there were times when Paul would sing with his understanding, in other words he would sing a song in his own native language, there were also times that he would sing praises to God in an unknown tongue that had been given to him by the Holy Spirit.

Indeed, on two of the three occasions in which people are recorded as speaking in tongues in the book of Acts, they are doing so as ways of praising God.

When the disciples spoke in tongues on the Day of Pentecost they were actually "declaring the wonders of God" (2:11) whilst the believers in Cornelius' household are specifically describing as praising God in tongues (10:46)

Colossians 3 gives us a further insight into how the New Testament Church sung their praises to God:

*"Let the message of Christ dwell among you richly as you teach and admonish one another with all wisdom through psalms, hymns, and songs from the Spirit, singing to God with gratitude in your hearts." (v16)*

There were three ways in which the first century church sung praises to God. One was using the Psalms – in other words they would sing the written scriptures. Another way was using hymns – these would be their contemporary songs and creeds. But another way they would sing praise was to sing "songs from the Spirit".

There are many wonderful songs of praise that have been written, but even the greatest of human song writers can fail to grasp how glorious and majestic God is. It is in those moments, when human language fails to grasp how great He is, that we begin to sing in tongues and release a song from the Spirit.

There are times when it can be helpful to sing words written for us by gifted poets and writers, but how much more powerful and intimate when I sing my own personal love song to Jesus, using words that no one around me can understand but He can!

There are also times when it doesn't make sense to praise God. I can look at my circumstances and my mind is telling me "what do you have to praise God for?" It is in those moments that I bypass my mind and begin to sign with my spirit using the gift of tongues.

Ephesians 5 again refers to this three-fold way of praising God using Psalms, hymns and spiritual songs but this time Paul tells us to "speak to one another" using these methods (v19).

What Paul is telling us here is that praising God, including praising Him in tongues, is not to be limited to just our own private devotional times but it is a powerful part of our corporate gatherings too. When we all sing together in a language we can understand there is wonderful unity in that moment, but also how glorious when many voices, all raised together, sing many songs in many different languages, not being restricted to words on a screen or hymn sheet, not being directed by a praise leader or band, but each of us individually being led by the Holy Spirit. In that moment all of us – not just the song leader – are being used to change the atmosphere and cause faith to arise.

In the previous verse to this, in Ephesians 5:18, Paul links singing in the Spirit to being filled with the Spirit.

The book of James compares the human tongue to the rudder of a ship. Whatever direction your tongue goes in, so goes your life.

If your tongue is evil, it sets you on a course to hell.

But if your tongue is controlled by the Holy Spirit what does it lead to? A life filled, led, directed, controlled and empowered by the Holy Spirit!

## Other benefits to tongues

*"Anyone who speaks in a tongue edifies themselves" (1 Corinthians 14:4)*

Praying in tongues is like going to a spiritual gymnasium! It helps you develop and strengthen your walk with Jesus. Praying in tongues builds you up in God. It strengthens you, encourages you and empowers you. If any part of your life is weak – speak in tongues. If your prayer life is weak – speak in tongues. If you don't feel particularly spiritual – speak in tongues.

In John 4, Jesus describes God's life in you as a spring of water that wells up to eternal life. A spring is a source of water, but it has to be drawn from. How do you draw water from a spring or a well? You lower your bucket or container into the water and bring it back to the surface full.

Praying and praising in tongues is like lowering your spiritual bucket into the spring of God's life that is often dormant within you. As you lower the bucket down and begin to exercise that spiritual gift, you are bringing to the surface joy, power, peace, healing and more as the life of the Spirit bubbles up from within you.

*"But you, dear friends, by building yourselves up in your most holy faith and praying in the Holy Spirit" (Jude v20)*

Praying in tongues builds up your faith. If you are filled with doubts or fear or are unsure of God's will in a situation, pray in tongues. Praying in tongues causes faith to arise. It gives you boldness and confidence in approaching God, in stepping out in ministry and in moving in the other gifts of the Spirit.

The believers at Ephesus who Paul encountered in Acts 19, had never even heard of the Holy Spirit and yet as soon as they spoke in tongues they began to prophesy! (v6). For them, speaking in tongues opened up for them the gift of prophesy. Many Christians who move in the prophetic or in gifts of healings or miracles will testify that speaking in tongues was the first spiritual gift they moved in. It seems like speaking in tongues is a gateway to the other gifts of the Spirit.

## Final thoughts

Speaking in tongues, like all spiritual manifestations, is a gift of the Holy Spirit. It cannot be earned or bought but can only be received. Understanding the goodness of the Father in wanting to give us His gifts (Luke 11:13) and then receiving in faith are the keys.

*Not only do we receive in faith, but we speak in tongues by faith: "these signs will accompany those who believe…they will speak in new tongues" (Mark 16:17)*

After praying in faith and receiving in faith, you have to open your mouth and speak in faith. In Acts 2, it was the disciples who spoke in tongues – not God controlling their mouths. They opened their mouths and spoke, as the Spirit enabled them. He does the enabling but we have to do the speaking!

Paul wrote to a younger believer called Timothy and urged him to "fan into flame the gracious gift of God, [that inner fire–the special endowment] which is in you" (2 Timothy 1:6 - Amp). I believe this idea of fanning into flame, or stirring up the fire that is in us, can again be done by praying and speaking in tongues.

When I think of stirring up the spirit, I am reminded of the Jewish tradition that took place around the pool of Bethesda.

Here a great number of disabled people used to lie – the blind, the lame, the paralysed. From time to time an angel of the Lord would come down and stir up the waters. The first one into the pool after each such disturbance would be cured of whatever disease they had. (John 5:3-4).

Whenever the angel stirred up the waters, an atmosphere for the miraculous was created. I believe that this is a powerful prophetic picture of what happens when we pray and sing in tongues in our church services. We are stirring the spiritual atmosphere and creating an environment where the sick can be healed and the miraculous can take place. We are building an atmosphere of faith where all things are possible.

Let's once again make speaking and singing in tongues an essential part of our devotional time and our church gatherings. Let's make being Pentecostal great again!

# About the Author

Andrew is the founder and director of Generation Builders and travels the world extensively as an evangelist, teacher and revivalist.

Born into a Christian family Andrew has been in full time Christian ministry since the age of eighteen. In September 2001 he began working full time at Royston Bethel Community Church in Barnsley, South Yorkshire. He remained on staff at the church for thirteen years serving initially as an intern and then later as a schools and youth worker.

During this time Andrew achieved a certificate in Biblical studies from Mattersey Hall Bible College and later became a fully accredited minister with the Assemblies of God UK and Ireland.

In 2006, Andrew was appointed youth pastor and then later assistant pastor at Bethel Church, serving firstly under Pastor John Morgan and later Pastor Dave Jones.

In January 2007 Andrew had a powerful encounter with the Holy Spirit which led to a wonderful move of God in the youth group at the church, with many young people coming and experiencing God's presence. This was the start of Andrew launching "Generation Builders" and beginning to travel to the nations.

In 2014 Andrew handed over his pastoral duties in the church and was released by the leadership to run Generation Builders full time. Since then he has travelled the world seeing moves of God's Spirit marked by salvations, healings and thousands of people impacted by the preaching and teaching of God's Word.

Andrew is currently on the leadership team at Revive Church, a multi-site church based in East Yorkshire led by Jarrod Cooper. Andrew ministers regularly at the church and also is the director of the Revive College training and equipping a new generation of revivalists.

Andrew is the author of three books including "Seeing The Church: When Your Purpose Collides with God's Passion" and "The Miracle Table: Rediscovering The Power Of Communion".

Andrew is married to Laura and they have two children Judah and Asher.

# Contact Information

For more information about "Generation Builders" ministries please visit our website www.generationbuilders.org

If you have been blessed by this book or are interested in having Andrew Murray speak at your church or event then please email admin@generationbuilders.org

For more information about our college and internship including how to apply then please visit www.revivechurch.co.uk

For more information about Peanut Designs please visit www.pnutd.co.uk

Other titles by Andrew Murray

# SEEING THE CHURCH
# &
# THE MIRACLE TABLE

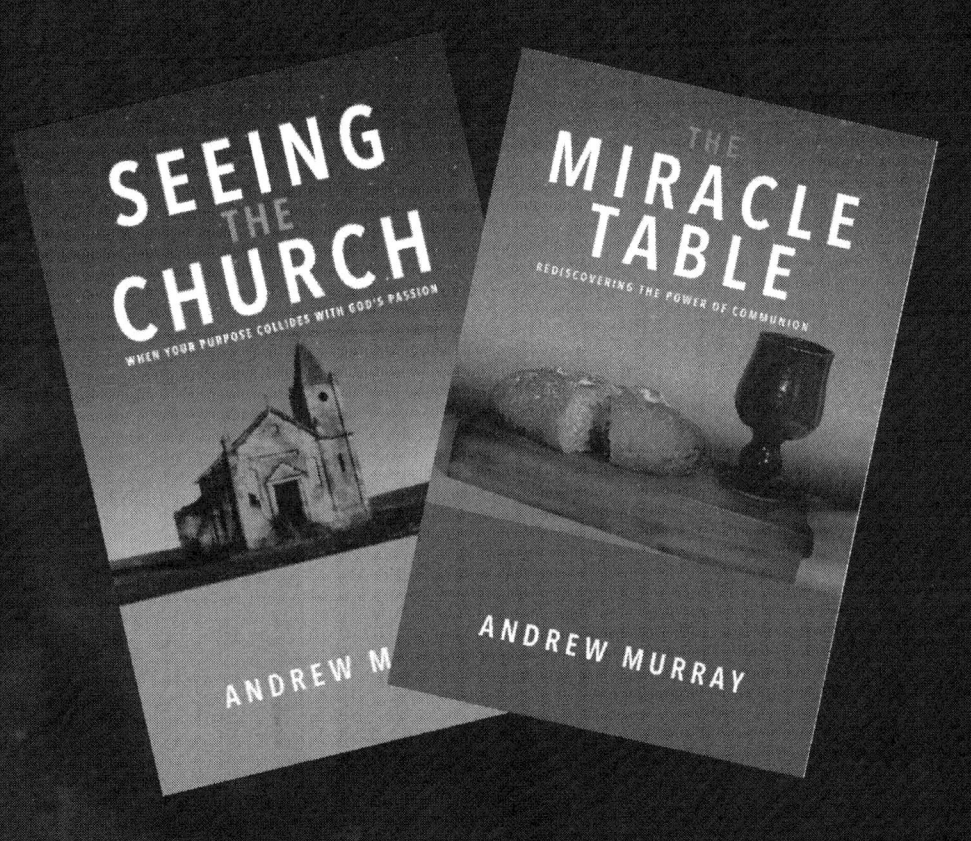

Available on
**amazon&kindle**

Printed in Poland
by Amazon Fulfillment
Poland Sp. z o.o., Wrocław